THE HERITAGE OF LIBRARIANSHIP SERIES,
No. 1

THE HERITAGE OF LIBRARIANSHIP SERIES

Michael H. Harris, General Editor

No. 1   *The Age of Jewett: Charles Coffin Jewett and American Librarianship, 1841-1868.* Edited by Michael H. Harris.

No. 2   *Ainsworth Rand Spofford: Bookman and Librarian.* Edited by John Y. Cole.

No. 3   *Charles Ammi Cutter.* Edited by Francis Miksa.

The Age of Jewett

CHARLES COFFIN JEWETT

and

American Librarianship, 1841-1868

edited by

MICHAEL H. HARRIS

Libraries Unlimited, Inc.   Littleton, Colo.

1975

LIBRARIES UNLIMITED, INC.
P.O. Box 263
Littleton, Colorado 80120

Library of Congress Cataloging in Publication Data

Jewett, Charles Coffin, 1816-1868.
   The age of Jewett.

   (The Heritage of librarianship series ; no. 1)
   Bibliography: p.
   Includes index.
   1. Libraries—United States—History—Sources.
2. Jewett, Charles Coffin, 1816-1868. I. Harris,
Michael H. II. Title. III. Title: Charles Coffin
Jewett and American librarianship, 1841-1868.
IV. Series.
Z731.J58   1975   020'.92'4 [B]   75-14205
ISBN 0-87287-113-4

For
Sidney Ditzion, Haynes McMullen,
Jesse Shera, and *Louis Shores*

Their research has provided a model
for several generations
of library historians

With this volume Libraries Unlimited inaugurates its Heritage of Librarianship Series. This series is designed to provide modern librarians, both here and abroad, with carefully selected collections of the writings of prominent American and European librarians. Each volume will also contain a substantive critical essay, written by a library historian, which will assess the subject's past and present significance to the profession of librarianship.

As the world's two oldest library associations approach their centennials—The American Library Association in 1976 and the Library Association (Great Britain) in 1977—it seems not only appropriate, but even necessary to pause and consider the historical development of the library profession. One way to do this is to examine the lives and accomplishments of a select number of prominent American and European librarians, men and women who reached positions of great influence, served with marked distinction in their own times, had a formative influence on the library profession, and have continued to exert influence on our day-to-day activities.

Far too few of these librarians have been afforded the serious and in-depth study they deserve. As a result, our understanding of their contributions, and consequently our understanding of the development of librarianship, is blurred and frequently distorted by myth and ideology.

All of the librarians considered in this series were prolific and persuasive writers who won with their pens much of their influence. And yet few modern librarians have any conception of what concerned them, what questions they sought to answer, or how they proposed to deal with their manifold problems. The Heritage of Librarianship Series will provide easy access to the writings of the world's most influential librarians and perhaps will facilitate in some small way the modern librarian's increasingly intensive search for the purpose of the library in a post-industrialized society.

It is easy enough to justify the choice of Charles Coffin Jewett as the subject for this first volume, for he was the first among his colleagues in an age that witnessed the first faint glimmerings of professional librarianship in America. He was the first man to hold a full-time post as academic librarian, the first librarian of what very nearly became the national library of the United States, the president of the first formal conference of librarians, and the first superintendent of the country's premier nineteenth century public library.

But Jewett too has suffered from neglect, and his pivotal significance in library history is often overlooked or misunderstood. Despite the appearance in the early 1950s of a short chronicle of his life (a volume in the abortive Library Pioneers series published by the American Library Association) and despite our fuller appreciation of his importance at the first conference of librarians (1853), he still remains an enigmatic and confusing figure.

It is hoped that this volume will provide librarians with some insight into the life and aspirations of a man who might well be considered the first "professional" American librarian. He was one who committed himself, at the risk of his health and ultimately his life, to the advancement of librarianship both here and abroad. In this volume Jewett speaks to the problems that demanded solution in his time and articulates the hopes and fears of his generation of librarians. Modern librarians will, we think, listen and be impressed by his foresight, commitment, and obvious grasp of the basic problems facing librarians both then and now.

A number of people contributed to the completion of this volume. Wayne Cutler, assistant editor of the *Papers of Henry Clay*, gave the manuscript a thorough review and contributed useful suggestions for its improvement. Jill Berkowsky, Patricia Boyle, Susan Broome, Kathy Connick, Nancy Dare, and Willa Harrelson all helped with the preparation of the manuscript.

M.H.H.
University of Kentucky
December 9, 1974

TABLE OF CONTENTS

FOREWORD   vii

PART I.   CHARLES COFFIN JEWETT
AND AMERICAN LIBRARIANSHIP

INTRODUCTION   3

EARLY LIFE AND EDUCATION   4

A CAREER CHOSEN: LIBRARIAN AT BROWN   11

A NATIONAL LIBRARY FOR THE UNITED STATES   20

THE LIBRARIANS' CONFERENCE OF 1853   33

TWILIGHT TIME: THE BOSTON PUBLIC LIBRARY   38

NOTES   44

PART II.   CHARLES COFFIN JEWETT ON BOOKS,
LIBRARIES AND LIBRARIANSHIP

THE PREFACE TO THE BROWN UNIVERSITY LIBRARY
       CATALOGUE OF 1843   59

FACTS AND CONSIDERATIONS RELATIVE
       TO DUTIES ON BOOKS   66

A NATIONAL LIBRARY FOR THE UNITED STATES 77

ON THE ACQUISITION OF BOOKS FOR THE
      NATIONAL LIBRARY 89

A NATIONAL UNION CATALOG OF AMERICAN
      LIBRARIES 98

THE CONTINUING DREAM OF A NATIONAL
      LIBRARY 104

ON LIBRARIANS AND CONFERENCES OF
      LIBRARIANS 112

JEWETT'S PRESIDENTIAL ADDRESS 116

THE SMITHSONIAN INSTITUTION AND ITS
      PLAN OF CATALOGING 120

ON THE CONSTRUCTION OF CATALOGUES 131

PART III: BIBLIOGRAPHY

JEWETT'S MANUSCRIPTS 159

JEWETT'S PUBLISHED WORKS 159

SECONDARY PUBLICATIONS 160

      INDEX 164

Part I

Charles Coffin Jewett
and American Librarianship

INTRODUCTION

Most librarians mark the beginning of modern librarianship from the founding of the American Library Association in 1876 and the appearance on the national library scene of such dynamic and controversial figures as Melvil Dewey and Charles Ammi Cutter.

But in doing so, they overlook an extremely significant era in the history of our profession, for the quarter century preceding the 1876 meeting in Philadelphia was one characterized by great advances in the field of American librarianship. This period of growth was to have considerable influence on the course of library development in America after 1876. To ignore the third quarter of the nineteenth century is to risk misinterpreting the pivotal post-1876 era, and in this time of reappraisal, it seems particularly appropriate and useful to focus our attention on the years preceding the founding of the American Library Association.

One way of probing this important precursor of that seminal period in American library history is to focus our attention on the man who was considered far and away the most prominent member of the emerging library profession. From the publication of his much heralded catalog of the Brown University Library in 1843, to the fatal attack of apoplexy which struck while he was at his desk in the Boston Public Library in 1868, Charles Coffin Jewett was the pivotal figure in American librarianship. His innovative practices in academic and public library administration were widely copied, and he was always consulted in matters of importance related to library operations. Only Dewey would come to command such a wide-ranging and strong influence on nineteenth-century American librarianship.

Thus, through a consideration of Jewett's life and published writings one gains significant insight into the age that witnessed the first stirrings of the library profession in America—The Age of Jewett, 1841-1868.

EARLY LIFE AND EDUCATION

Charles Coffin Jewett was born on 12 August 1816, the son of Paul Jewett and Eleanor Masury Punchard Jewett.[1] Paul Jewett, representing the sixth generation of Jewetts to call themselves Americans, was a young minister in Lebanon, Maine.

Charles Coffin's father was well educated, having earned his degree at Brown in 1802, and he had served successfully as a tutor at his alma mater from 1806 to 1809. Indeed, his teaching was deemed so successful that in his last year he was offered the equivalent of tenure in a modern university, but in a pattern not uncommon to his day, he resolved to devote his life to the church, declined the offer made by the Trustees, and set about preparing for the ministry.

In 1812, amid the turmoil and anguish of the war just begun between Great Britain and America—derisively referred to in New England as "Mr. Madison's War"—he responded to a call from the Congregational Church in Lebanon, Maine. Despite depressing news from the battlefields and increasing public alienation against the conflict, Reverend Jewett's first years in the pulpit appear to have been filled with achievement and passed in relative tranquility.

In 1813, he married Eleanor Masury Punchard, a native of Salem, Massachusetts; and in the next year she presented him with a son, John Punchard Jewett, who was later to gain considerable fame as the man who published *Uncle Tom's Cabin*.[2] The year 1814 also marked a most important time in the young minister's life; it was the year he was ordained to the pastoral care of the church.

For a time the Jewett family prospered and grew. Charles Coffin was born in 1816, and George Baker, in 1818. But in the following year Reverend Jewett encountered difficulties with the church council which advised him to withdraw from his post. The hard days of the depression then gripping much of the country made it all the more difficult to accept his dismissal; nevertheless, he moved his family to Salem.

Reverend Jewett's family was blessed in 1820 with the birth of a fourth son, Henry Paul, but this joy was followed quickly by a time of great sadness, as first his beloved wife, and then his youngest son were taken by death. Paul Jewett's life was afflicted during subsequent years by an unstable and almost frantic existence, as he moved from one church to another. He was suddenly, and finally, stopped by an attack of apoplexy in 1840.

Despite the unsettled circumstances of his family during his youth, Charles Coffin received the benefits of a good education. As a result, he was graduated from the Salem Latin School in 1831; and, like his father before him, he enrolled at Dartmouth (Rhode Island) College and then quickly transferred to Brown.

When Charles Coffin arrived at Brown he must have been awed by the city of Providence, which had experienced tremendous growth since 1820. Responding to the post-depression commercial, transportation, and industrial boom, large numbers of people, many of them poor and illiterate Blacks and Irish, were moving into the city and clustering together in ghetto areas in dangerous concentrations. This situation contributed to a general instability in society, and as a result of the inability of the city fathers to deal effectively with such problems, the times were heavily freighted with tension. Nevertheless, the citizenry was at once shocked and horrified by a ferocious riot that broke out on 21 September 1831.[3]

Never had the city experienced such violence and bloodshed. The riot began on Olney Street between white sailors and poor Blacks, and for five days the racial strife intensified. On the sixth day the "great crowd," determined to destroy the Black shanty town, confronted the state's militia, led by Governor Lemuel Hastings Arnold, who addressed the rioters and ordered them to disperse. When they failed to do so, the strained nerves of the militia men reached a breaking point. Several volleys of shot dispersed the mob, killing four and wounding many others.[4]

The community was stunned by the tragic events, but everyone in a position of authority agreed that the action was justified in the face of the "open and lawless attack upon private property." A commission of 14 distinguished citizens was impaneled and in due time reported, noting that "of all the evils that can be inflicted upon civil society, that of a lawless and ferocious mob is the most capricious in its objects, the most savage in its means, and the most extensive in its consequences."[5]

The press and the pulpits were full of calls for a return to law and order, and the immediate cry was for a strengthened police force. How the young students at Brown reacted to this affair is generally unknown. However, ten years later Charles Coffin Jewett, then a young professor at Brown, would echo the sentiments expressed in Providence, but this time he would be decrying "Dorr's mob."[6]

While the tumultuous affairs in Providence certainly made some impression on the young scholar, the matter of his studies must have been foremost in his mind. Charles Coffin Jewett was fortunate in attending Brown during the tenure of its brilliant and controversial president, Francis Wayland.

Wayland, a strict disciplinarian and a vigorous academician, was gaining a reputation as an innovator in academic affairs. This fact, coupled with his enormous reputation as the nation's most widely known and most widely read moral philosopher, led each new student to look forward with excitement to meeting and studying under the great man.[7]

Jewett appears to have had a particular interest in languages, and such a penchant was amply cultivated by the curriculum at Brown. The University's curriculum, despite Wayland's ideas about reform, remained that of a classical college committed to the study and assimilation of those few subjects which had formed the basic curriculum from colonial times. Course work included Latin, Greek, logic, mathematics, and "moral philosophy," with some attention to modern foreign languages and elementary physical sciences.[8]

The curriculum, as announced in the catalog of 1842-43, is representative of the years Jewett spent at Brown and thus reveals the nature of Jewett's preparation for professional life.

FRESHMAN YEAR

First Term. Plane geometry; Livy; Latin grammar reviewed; abstract of Roman history; Xenophon's Cyropaedia; Greek grammer reviewed.

Second Term. Solid geometry; algebra; Livy, abstract of Roman history; exercises in writing Latin; Xenophon's Memorabilia; exercises in writing Greek.

Third Term. Algebra; Tacitus, exercises in writing Latin; the Odyssey; exercises in writing Greek.

SOPHOMORE YEAR

First Term. Algebra; plane and spherical trigonometry; Horace; exercises in writing Latin; the Iliad; exercises in writing Greek.

Second Term. Mensuration, surveying, navigation, nautical astronomy; the Iliad; exercises in writing Greek; Horace; rhetoric.

Third Term. Analytical geometry; de Amicitia and de Senectute; exercises in writing Latin; rhetoric; Euripides.

JUNIOR YEAR

First Term. Mechanics; animal physiology; logic; modern languages.

Second Term. Pneumatics and hydrostatics; chemistry; Sophocles or Aeschylus; modern languages.

Third Term. Optics; chemistry; vegetable physiology; Juvenal; modern languages.

SENIOR YEAR

First Term. Intellectual philosophy; astronomy; Aeschines or Demosthenes; modern languages.

Second Term. Moral philosophy; Butler's Analogy and Paley's Evidences; rhetoric; modern languages.

Third Term. Political economy; evidences of Christianity; geology; American constitution; modern languages.[9]

Charles Coffin Jewett appears to have developed a keen interest in books early in life, and this love of books, coupled with his lack of personal fortune, made him a ready user of libraries.[10] Upon arrival at Brown he found a library that, like those of the other colonial colleges, was poorly suited for the needs of a reader with voracious and wide-ranging interests. Despite the efforts of President Wayland to build a fund designed to support the library at an adequate level, the collection numbered only about 6,000 volumes in 1833.[11]

Fortunately, Jewett had recourse to several fine literary society libraries at Brown. These societies, like their counterparts in most of the colleges in America, were primarily debating societies; their interests ranged across all areas of academic and public concern. Since these debates were expected to be learned, as well as rhetorically correct, the students immediately recognized the need for substantial libraries from which to mine their material.

The college library of the antebellum period offered little support for the contemporary and popular reading interests of the society members and inflexibly adhered to prohibitive use regulations. As a result, the societies quickly developed libraries that in many cases rivaled or completely excelled their respective college libraries in size and usefulness.[12]

At Brown, the leading society was the Philermenian, founded as the Miskosmian Society in 1794, and reorganized and renamed in 1798. The members of the Philermenian gathered for fortnightly meetings to listen to debates, to hear their fellows read speeches and poems, and to judge declamations. In 1798 the society began to collect a library, and by 1821 it contained 1,594 well-selected volumes. These books were housed in the college "library room" until 1823, when they were transferred to the new home of the society in Hope College.[13]

It was in this library that Jewett gained his first actual "professional experience" and began to develop a specialty that was to become his greatest contribution to librarianship. For, during his student days, he and a classmate,

William Lawton Brown, cataloged and arranged the books belonging to the society and placed them securely in the cases lining the society library.[14]

Jewett graduated from Brown in 1835, the youngest member of his class, and promptly acquired a position at the Uxbridge, Massachusetts, Academy. There he served quietly until he felt the call to prepare for the ministry—a call felt and heeded by many of his peers—and decided to enter Andover Seminary in 1837.

Charles Coffin Jewett chose to pursue his religious studies at the nation's premier theological seminary. Americans familiar with the contemporary theological seminary are likely to underestimate Andover's significance in its own day. As J. Earl Thompson points out in a paper on Andover, the seminaries provided a prototype for post-graduate education, thus constituting an important prelude to the emergence of the modern university.[15]

Andover stood preeminent among these schools, and its excellent library and three-year program provided the opportunity for young scholars of superior ability to develop their talents under conditions most conducive to that development.

But while Andover ranked as the nation's foremost graduate school, it must be quickly noted that it was not a particularly innovative or progressive institution. Indeed, for the first three-quarters of a century of its history, 1806 to 1881, Andover ranked as the strongest advocate of the Calvinist tradition in New England. Young scholars of Jewett's day were admonished to "put on the harness"—that is, to live a Christian life of "practical morality and piety" as dictated by the seminary leadership.[16] This commitment was viewed as having two basic components: active participation in religious activities, and cultivation of such personal qualities as temperance and brotherly love.

Great emphasis was placed on conversion, and Andover men were prominent in the two movements most appropriate to this focus: revivalism and missionary work. Thus, it comes as no surprise to find graduates of the school playing significant roles in the "revival seasons" of 1837 and 1857, while at the same time providing all but one of the missionaries sent out by the American Board of Commissioners for Foreign Missions in its first ten years of existence.

The course of study was vigorous and carefully disciplined, with each student being publicly examined each year by faculty, trustees, and visitors. Students were insulated as much as possible from potentially disturbing experiences and ideas, and doctrine was "hammered in."[17]

Consistently the faculty and trustees emphasized the fact that the primary business of the church was with individuals' souls. Anything that hindered this all-consuming emphasis was to be deplored.

This insistence on the scholarly and Christian nature of Andover led to one of the most celebrated cases in the school's history. In the mid-thirties, abolitionist leaders attempted to organize the seminarians and the Andover faculty for the crusade against slavery.[18]

However, the faculty, true to their commitment to eschew such involvement, recommended that the students reject the abolitionist proposal.

Consequently the students prepared a public statement which they released to the press:

> While connected with the Seminary, our duties as Theological Students have the first claim upon our attention; and fearing that the agitation of the subject of slavery might interfere with the vigorous prosecution of our studies, and with that harmony that ought to prevail among us; We therefore disapprove for the present of all associated action on the subject, in this institution.[19]

The objective was to avoid "contentious moral reforms," especially anti-slavery agitation with its dangerous and untenable call for "immediate and violent disruption, at all hazards." Such a course would be ruinous for the nation and should be avoided at all cost.[20]

But while the faculty and students were adamant in their refusal to contribute to social instability and general unrest, they moved with vigor to support reforms that might contribute to stability and social order. Thus they were active proponents of temperance in the thirties and forties. As Thompson points out, what the seminarians "were willing to do publicly and privately for white drunks, they were unwilling to do for Black slaves."[21] It was to an Andover bound by the basic tenets of patience, piety, stability, and temperance that Jewett directed himself in 1837. A dedicated student, he excelled at Andover and continued to cultivate his interest in languages, especially "Oriental languages and Eastern Antiquities." As time passed his interest in the latter increased to the point where he decided to travel to the Orient upon graduation in order to study the subject further.

While a student at Andover, Jewett was offered a second opportunity to catalog a library. Professor Oliver A. Taylor invited him to assist in the preparation of the soon-to-be-famous *1838 Catalogue of the Andover Theological Seminary Library*.[22]

Taylor's efforts were complicated by the confused nature of cataloging practice of the day. As Ranz points out, those charged with the responsibility of cataloging a library collection faced a number of serious problems related to questions of the arrangement, determination, and nature of entries.[23]

Taylor and others were particularly aware of the need to provide an alphabetical author-title list of books in the library, while at the same time offering the user some kind of subject approach to the collection. In the days before the widespread adoption of the dictionary catalog arrangement, this problem loomed large in the minds of catalogers.

Taylor and his young assistant overcame the first part of this problem by preparing a printed catalog designed "to exhibit a full and perfect alphabetical description of everything the library contains."[24] They intended to resolve the second difficulty by appending a "Systematic Index" to the alphabetical catalog. This index, if patterned after the "Systematic Index" pioneered by Benjamin Pierce in 1830 for the Harvard University *Catalogue*, would have been arranged under five or six large classes with numerous subdivisions, and with entries arranged alphabetically within each sequence.[25] However, the index was never published.

Nevertheless, Taylor's catalog exhibited remarkable skill and knowledge and stands out as a landmark in the history of cataloging in this country. Those examining it were very favorably impressed by the effort devoted to locating and identifying authors; the superb system of cross references and added entries; and the precise and accurate nature of the bibliographical descriptions. All of these characteristics, plus the inclusion of biographical notices on authors and frequent bibliographical descriptions of their works, were to become hallmarks of the Jewett catalogs that appeared in later years.

Indeed, in the preface to his famous Brown University Library *Catalogue* of 1843, Jewett acknowledged the extent of his intellectual debt to Taylor. He testified to the value of his tutelage under his old mentor when he wrote:

> In the arrangement of the Catalogue I have followed the plan of Mr. O. A. Taylor's Catalogue of the Library of the Theological Seminary in Andover, Mass.; a work far superior to all others of this kind, which have been published in this country, and which has been pronounced in Germany a *model for a Catalogue*. I have found my own labors considerably abridged by the use of this accurate work.

Jewett's library experience at Brown and Andover, coupled with his increasing familiarity with bibliographical affairs and his obvious scholarly attributes, admirably qualified him for the profession he was soon to enter and serve with distinction.[26] That profession suddenly opened to him in the autumn of 1841, when he accepted the position as Librarian at Brown University.

A CAREER CHOSEN:
LIBRARIAN AT BROWN

*Chance Aggregations of
the Gifts of Charity*

The college libraries of Jewett's time were characterized by small collections, cramped quarters, and part-time help. Generally, a member of the faculty was charged with the responsibility for supervising the library, a task one was expected to assume with no reduction in other duties and no increase in pay.[27]

As a result, one is not surprised to find that these new "librarians" were often reluctant recruits who approached their duties with distaste and impatience. Consequently, hours when the library was open for use were short; rules were strict and inflexible; and the librarian was often viewed with mixed emotions of fear and disgust by the students.

In 1841, the Brown University Library numbered some 10,000 volumes and ranked as one of the better collections in the country. However, President Wayland's consistent and enlightened support of the library, coupled with the generosity of the school's alumni, made the position of Librarian at Brown one of the most prized in America.

Wayland had shown genuine concern for the inadequate and "miscellaneous character" of the library as early as 1827 and had soon set about raising a library fund of $25,000, the interest from which would be utilized for the acquisition of books. This fund, amazing as it seemed at the time, was successfully raised; and after 1839, it provided $500 annually for the library budget.

The availability of a sizable annual book fund, a rarity in those days, was only one of the factors that would have encouraged the new librarian. Another attractive feature of the situation at Brown was the recently completed library. This facility, housed on the ground floor of Manning Hall, completed in 1835, was spacious, well-lit, and capable of holding 30,000 volumes without serious crowding.

Finally, President Wayland had expressed his interest in increasing student use of the library, and he was the type of administrator who would welcome—indeed, insist upon—innovation and sound management. This perhaps explains his willingness to break with tradition and appoint the country's first full-time academic librarian at a salary of $600 a year.

And so Charles Coffin Jewett entered the library profession under the most favorable of conditions. During his years as Librarian at Brown, he achieved many small successes; but his day-to-day achievements are over-shadowed by two major accomplishments: the appearance of his landmark *Catalogue of the Brown University Library* in 1843, and his astounding book-buying tour of Europe in 1844-45. These two activities, which had such an obvious formative influence on his life, will be discussed at some length later. First, however, we must examine a socio-political event in Rhode Island's history which, due to Jewett's involvement, provides us with a rare insight into the nature of his beliefs and the development of his character.

God Frustrated the Designs
of These Wicked Men

The obvious and welcome advantages of Jewett's new position were somewhat eclipsed in 1842 by the gathering storm clouds of the Dorr War. This rebellion, one of the classic examples of American radicalism, broke out in the summer of 1842, although its origins went back for many years.[28] The Dorr War itself erupted when a large group of disenfranchised mechanics, journeymen, and younger sons of farmers grew exasperated in the face of the state government's repeated refusal to give them the right to vote. Led by Thomas W. Dorr, they rebelled, formed a new state government, and attempted to impose their "People's Constitution" upon the state. As Marvin Gettleman points out, they also "developed a radical ideology that at key points challenged the dominant values of antebellum society and implied that vast political and social changes might be necessary."[29]

Such a challenge, of course, could not go unanswered, and Rhode Island conservatives and moderates alike entered the lists in opposition to the Dorrites and their violent and impatient methods. Some of the foremost advocates of law and order were members of the Brown University staff.

Most significant was President Wayland himself, a man long identified with educational reform and one who prided himself in having among his friends "the rich and the poor, of every sect and all parties." Wayland, like many other social and intellectual leaders in the state, readily admitted that he had "always been in favor of the extension of suffrage"; but the violent behavior of Dorr and his band of "ignorant and abandoned men" led him to take to the pulpit of the First Baptist Church of Providence and decry the behavior of this wild and lawless man who threatened the social and moral order of the community.[30] For Wayland, as for so many of his conservative colleagues at Brown, the impatient and anarchic behavior of the Dorrites and the threat their behavior constituted for the Republic now supplanted entirely the issue of political liberty that originally precipitated the crisis.

Another Brown faculty member to speak out vigorously on this matter was William Goddard, Professor of Moral Philosophy and a man much more conservative than Wayland. Goddard was among a group of vocal conservatives who opposed suffrage reform because it promised to extend the right to vote to those who had no "stake in society" and thus would not make "wise and judicious voters and governors." Such a step, argued the conservatives, would lead "straight away to anarchy, and ultimately to despotism." If the "idle and ignorant" people gained power the government of Rhode Island would no longer be characterized by reason, justice, and morality; but rather, it would reflect the violent and selfish interests of the "dram shop, the brothel, and the gutter." Eventually the Republic would falter and then crumble into ruins.[31]

How did librarian Jewett view these developments? His background, his education, his personality, and his devout commitment to his religion and to high moral standards combined to make him come out strongly in opposition to the rebels. In 1842 his concern for the situation overcame his basic passivity, and he actually took up arms against the rebels, noting: "men who move not on ordinary occasions were out, to sustain the law and protect the people."[32]

The Librarian found the impudent and violent challenge to legitimate and moral authority by the modern day "Cataline" to be so excessive as to require resistance, and in an anonymous pamphlet "on the Late Rebellion ... by a Massachusetts Man Resident in Providence," he exploded into polemical fireworks against the Dorrites.

After describing at length the events in Providence when the rebels under Dorr attempted unsuccessfully to storm the arsenal and were driven in shame from the city, he noted that "this contest" proves "that no political end is to be gained here by resort to threats and violence. . . ."[33]

The point was clear; "all sensible men ... know full well that they can easily obtain all they desire by peaceable and constitutional measures." But the outcome had been in question, for he said, "I thought I could see the interests of rational liberty throughout the United States, depending on the issue."[34]

And then in a revealing summary he lectured:

> It teaches a most salutary lesson to the whole country. In getting up this excitement, every art of demagogueism and deception was plied to the utmost ... the only *real* object was to bring a few broken down political outcasts again into power.[35]

Further, he said, only the "Tammany Hall agitators, the Slamm Jacobins, the reckless demagogues, the cormorants that scream for plunder near every battle field, were ready to adopt this misbegotten bantling and rear it into a champion to fight them into power." It was obvious that "respectable men of every party would have nothing to do with it."[36]

But in the final analysis, "it was God who frustrated the designs of these wicked men—to Him should be rendered the praise."[37] And so we recover a glimpse of Jewett, the man—devout, bound by strict morality, committed to obedience of legitimate authority as a central tenet of Republican government, and horrified by threats of violence and anarchy.

A Library without a Catalogue
Is like a Body without an Eye

And so amid the violence and turmoil of Dorr's rebellion, Jewett launched his career as a "professional librarian."[38] Despite his own assessment of the collection as "very miscellaneous" and despite his strong desire to remedy the "obvious deficiencies" in "nearly every department," he turned instead to a long and difficult task, that of preparing a catalog for the collection.[39]

Two printed catalogs of the Library's holdings had been previously issued. The first, completed in 1793, listed some 2,173 volumes, while the second, completed in 1826, demonstrated that the collection had grown to 5,818 volumes. In 1841 the Library contained some 10,235 bound volumes, 416 of which were pamphlets.

Due to the interest of the school's President, and the generosity of the friends of the institution, the promise of rapid growth seemed certain to be fulfilled. As Jewett noted in the preface to his 1843 *Catalogue*:

> The generosity of the friends of the College had furnished it with a good nucleus for a Library, and had also provided a fund for its regular and rapid increase; but, from the necessity of the case, scarcely any labor had been bestowed upon the Library for the purpose of rendering its treasures more available. It became obvious to the Committee entrusted with the care of this department, that in order to the perfect accomplishment of the object of the subscribers to the Fund, the Library must be newly arranged and catalogued.[40]

As noted earlier, Jewett was admirably qualified for the job of preparing the new catalog. His work as a student cataloger at Brown and Andover and, most importantly, his experience working on Taylor's catalog of the Andover Library collection, were to prove very useful to him in his present task.

Jim Ranz, in his study of the printed book catalog in American libraries during this period, points out that such catalogs were issued soon after academic libraries were established at Harvard, William and Mary, and Yale. At first these printed lists were designed as promotional items and frequently they were arranged by author, and not infrequently by size![41]

However, in time, those charged with the responsibility of organizing library collections for use began to view the catalog as a finding tool and bibliographic reference tool.[42] Now questions relating to selection and format of entries, and to the arrangement of entries once established, became central; and in the first half of the nineteenth century, these questions were both perplexing and controversial. There was as yet little standardization in practice, and each library had its own unique approach to the problems of cataloging. One librarian only slightly exaggerated the case in 1850 when he noted:

> there are no problems in art or science that have been found more perplexing in practice, or more incapable of a satisfactory theoretical solution. . . . Men have become insane in their efforts to reduce these labors to a system; and several instances are recorded where life has been sacrificed in consequence of the mental and physical exertion required for the completion of a catalogue in accordance with the author's view of the proper method of executing the task.[43]

Jewett's solutions to the problems facing catalogers in mid-century America were to have widespread and lasting influence; but they too were accomplished at great cost in time and energy—a cost, he noted, that "none will appreciate . . . but those who have been engaged in similar labors, and they will estimate it aright, without any remarks of mine."[44]

Jewett's description of his methods for cataloging the Brown University Library collection is reprinted in this volume. However, it remains for us to estimate the impact of his catalog on cataloging practice and to attempt to understand the reasons for the work's widespread acceptance.

Taylor's influence of Jewett's new catalog is obvious, not only upon careful analysis of the catalog itself, but also in his pointed acknowledgment of the usefulness of the Andover model. As Jewett noted in the preface, the *Catalogue* consisted of two parts: an alphabetically arranged "descriptive" catalog of all the books in the Library and an alphabetically arranged "Index of Subjects." This approach constituted a conclusive break with the tradition of preparing catalogs arranged by some logical classification, and the addition of an alphabetical subject index was instrumental in the evolution of a catalog made up of one alphabetical sequence containing author, title, and subject entries— that is, the modern dictionary catalog.[45]

Thus his influence was great in the area of catalog arrangement; but it was also felt in the areas of the nature and format of entry. It was Jewett who demonstrated very persuasively the value of producing a catalog that could serve as both a finding aid and a bibliographic reference tool.[46] His inclusion of biographical notices on many authors and bibliographical notes on their works set a pattern that was to characterize cataloging practice for years to come.

Modern-day catalogers, laboring as they do in relative obscurity, even among their own colleagues, will be puzzled by the widespread attention awarded to Jewett's *Catalogue*, once it was published. Several lengthy reviews appeared in major literary journals, and Jewett's *Catalogue* was the center of attention among his colleagues in the nascent library profession.

One of the most impressive notices was published in the prestigious *North American Review* in January of 1844. This article, some ten pages long, is devoted to a review of the library situation in America, and more specifically, to the Brown University Library and its new *Catalogue*. The reviewer, after noting the embarrassing weaknesses of American academic libraries due mainly to "the absurd multiplication of academical institutions in this country," turns to a detailed and highly informed analysis of the *Catalogue*.[47]

Jewett must have been pleased to see his catalog praised as "one of the most skillfully prepared and beautifully executed works of its class," and probably was not bothered by the prophetic, but qualified, conclusion: "on the whole, he has produced a valuable book, and we only regret, that his eminent qualifications for the task were not tested by the preparation of one of much greater extent."[48] One can only guess that the reviewer would have viewed Jewett's "National Union Catalogue" idea, formulated a decade later, as more appropriate to his talents.

Thus, after two years of difficult and lonely work, Jewett had completed the task of cataloging the Brown University Library collection and had done so with a success that must have astounded even the most sanguine of observers. His reputation was now firmly established; his star was definitely on the ascent; and he was being ranked among the most prominent librarians of his day. Having now a place among the country's leading library organizers, he was soon to have the opportunity to establish a reputation as one of the most knowledgeable and aggressive bookmen in the nation.

The Judicious Use of a
Few Thousand Dollars

The anonymous reviewer of Jewett's *Catalogue* had prefaced his remarks on the work in question with some provocative and well-informed comments on libraries in America. He was quite specific about academic library collections; and he noted that most of these collections were of an unbalanced nature, being made up primarily of books donated to the respective libraries. Then he stated what has become a paradigm of library administration:

> a collection of books made up almost exclusively from private benefactions, accumulating during a long period of years, cannot be so valuable as one of even quite inferior size, obtained by the direct expenditure of a considerable sum at one time, with due regard to the selection of the works which are most needed.[49]

However, the situation promised to be markedly improved in the future, for:

> The cost of books has been much diminished of late years, and the facilities for making large collections of them much increased. The recent improvements in the arts of printing and paper-making, and the great increase in the number of readers and purchasers, enabling the trade to count upon extensive sales, cause new works to be offered at very low prices; while the frequent dispersion of private libraries, after the death of the person whose taste and liberality

collected them, and, in the Old World, the multiplication of book-fairs and reprints, and the formation of large repositories of old books on sale, place nearly all the old and standard publications within the reach of very moderate means.[50]

He concluded, by noting in a prophetic fashion, that "the judicious use of a few thousand dollars will now furnish the nucleus of a very respectable collection of books."

That very year, Charles Coffin Jewett was to launch a book-buying expedition that would prove this statement remarkably accurate. Having completed the pressing task of cataloging the library collection, Jewett accepted the position of Professor of Modern Languages and Literature while agreeing to continue as Librarian.

Accompanying the offer of the new position was the promise of a European trip designed to allow the scholar-librarian to study modern languages and literature, while at the same time buying books for the library and making contact with European librarians in order to study their methods.

London, Paris, Berlin, Frankfort, Leipzig, Rome—all "the large repositories of old books on sale" were visited, and Jewett achieved unprecedented success in the "judicious use of a few thousand dollars." When he returned to America in December of 1845, he was able to report the acquisition of some 7,021 books purchased at an average cost of $1.20 a volume—that figure included binding and "other expenses of every kind up to the time of shipping."[51] This feat was to become the topic of conversation among bibliophiles everywhere, and it placed Jewett in the company of scholar-bookmen like Joseph Green Cogswell, George Ticknor, and Henry Stevens.

One of Jewett's principal reasons for going abroad was to meet leading European librarians and to learn what he could of European library practice. It was in this pursuit that Jewett came under the influence of Antonio Panizzi, the flamboyant and controversial Keeper of Printed Books of the British Museum.[52]

Jewett was, like so many others, completely taken by Panizzi, and quickly came to view him as the "Prince of Librarians." In a letter written some years later, Jewett remembered his trip abroad:

> . . . after having been employed for several years as a Librarian, and having thus become familiar with all the details of a Librarian's duties, I spent two years on the continent of Europe, visiting the principal libraries, for the purpose of collecting such information as would enable us in America to establish our libraries on the best possible foundation. With this preparation I went to England. You know how much time I spent at the British Museum, and how kindly and courteously we were both received by all the gentlemen connected with the establishment. The opinion which I formed, and which I believe I expressed to Mr. Panizzi, I still hold,—that any person who wishes to become thoroughly acquainted with the whole subject of *Bibliothekswissenschaft* (to use a German term for which we have no English equivalent), with the science of libraries,—need

go no farther than the British Museum. In my opinion, it is by far the best-regulated library in the world. The books are more faithfully guarded, and the public are more promptly served, than in any other library with which I am acquainted.[53]

Jewett was particularly impressed with the national character of the library, and Panizzi's concept of its role in England must certainly have played a part in the formation of Jewett's thoughts on the need for a similar institution in this country.

Once home, Jewett served with success in his dual role as scholar-librarian at Brown. He is remembered as a teacher of great knowledge, who enjoyed both teaching and students.[54]

I Would Most Respectfully Suggest . . .
Immediate and Energetic Efforts
to Repeal All Duties upon Books

In the library he continued to develop the collection and increasingly began to view his role in the library profession in national terms. This fact is demonstrated by his reaction to the Walker Tariff of 1846, which among other things proposed to place an ad valorem duty of 20 percent upon most books imported into the country. Jewett, in a pamphlet entitled *Facts and Considerations Relative to Duties on Books*, articulated a view that has become the librarians' creed, but that was in his own time a forceful and rarely heard argument for removing all artificial obstacles to the free flow of information in a democratic society.[55]

Jewett began his argument by noting that the duty would do little to augment the revenue of the nation, but rather "it must be obvious to anyone at all familiar with the subject, that the number [of books] imported would be greatly diminished."[56] He then presented an argument that demonstrated his informed and realistic view of the nature of reading in America:

It should be remembered that there is a radical difference between the demand for books, or of food for the mind, and of food for the body. The latter cannot be dispensed with, and the demand for it will be comparatively constant, even though high duties be imposed upon it. The former, however, can be dispensed with, and the demand will diminish as the taxes increase.[57]

Further he noted, remembering his recent trip to Europe, the duty "would render it impossible for our literary institutions to avail themselves of the frequent opportunities, which occur at the book-auctions of Europe, to procure for our public libraries, at a trifling price, the literary treasures of other nations and past ages."[58]

He then turned to a discussion of the reasons the lack of a duty on books would not hurt two groups intensely interested in it: American authors and publishers. The argument is of considerable interest and is reprinted in the second half of this book; but Jewett's concluding statement deserves quotation here:

> But there is one consideration on this subject, which is the most important of all, and which shows that the interests of the community, of authors, and of publishers, are identical; and that all would be injured by restrictions, of any sort, upon the importation of books. It is simply this, that the interests of all are promoted by a taste for reading. Everything that tends to promote such a taste, is subject for mutual congratulation, and everything which discourages it, injures all alike. It is too trite a truism to be gravely uttered, that the diffusion of knowledge is a benefit to the community. . . .
>
> A love for learning, and a taste for reading, are progressive and insatiable. They grow by what they feed on. . . . Our community is, just now, in a forming state. A taste for reading must be developed. People must learn by experience how pleasant and useful a thing it is to read. To this end, they must be furnished with good books. They must, too, be furnished with them *cheap*, for so engrossed are we here with material pursuits, that we are not willing to pay much for pleasures, purely mental, which, as yet, we have hardly learned to prize.[59]

And then, just before closing, he returns to the matter of national pride. European libraries, he points out, are rich beyond imagination. "But we do not possess, in all our public libraries combined, books enough to meet the wants of a thorough scholar in any one of the great departments of human learning."[60]

Continuing, he urges "the Library Committee . . . to prevent any increase of the present duties, and, if possible, to secure—so far as it can be done consistently with the affording of a reasonable protection to American publishers, a repeal of all duties on books." His argument appears as one of the first and most articulate of many made by librarians determined to defend the interest of readers against the self-interested proponents of duties or copyright restrictions that would inhibit the free and ready access to information so essential to the successful functioning of a democracy.

His growing awareness of the role of the professional librarian as both conservator of the national heritage and advocate for readers everywhere, combined with his unrivaled reputation as scholar and administrator, almost foreordained that Charles Coffin Jewett should become librarian at the Smithsonian Institution. For the Smithsonian promised to become both the "National Library" so necessary in the eyes of literary nationalists, and the vehicle designed to satisfy Jewett's ambition to bring system and leadership to the emerging library field.

A NATIONAL LIBRARY
FOR THE UNITED STATES

On the 26th day of June in 1829, a well-known English chemist named James Smithson died in Genoa. The terms of his will provided for what at first was viewed as a potential white elephant, but soon proved to be a magnificent legacy to the United States.[61] The will, written in 1826, left the majority of his estate to a nephew, Henry James Hungerford, stipulating that Henry was to receive only the income from the property; and then came the thunderbolt:

> In the case of the death of my said Nephew without leaving a child or children, or the death of the child or children he may have had under the age of twenty-one years or intestate, I then bequeath the whole of my property, subject to the Annuity of One Hundred pounds to John Fitall, ... to the United States of America, to found in Washington, under the name of the Smithsonian Institution, an Establishment for the increase and diffusion of knowledge among men. . . .[62]

Six years later Henry Hungerford died without children, and the Congress of the United States was informed by President Andrew Jackson that the bequest had been made:

Washington, December 17, 1835
To the Senate and House of Representatives of the United States
I transmit to Congress a report from the Secretary of State, accompanying copies of certain papers relating to a bequest to the United States by Mr. James Smithson, of London, for the purpose of founding at Washington an establishment . . . "for the increase and diffusion of knowledge among men." The Executive having no authority to take any steps for accepting the trust and obtaining the funds, the papers are communicated with a view to such measures as Congress may deem necessary.[63]

For several years Congress was "seized" of a series of proposals concerning the disposition of the Smithson bequest. These proposals ranged from the suggestion of Anglophobes that the money should be returned to Great Britain forthwith to the fairly popular idea that the money might be spent on a great observatory or university.

Despite much discussion and some rather heated debate, the Congress made little headway until 1844, when Benjamin Tappen, Senator from Ohio, introduced Senate Bill 18 in December. This bill was to become, after some amendment, the organizing act for the Smithsonian Institution.

Tappen's bill stipulated early in the text that one of the Institution's objectives should be the "purchase of books . . . *Provided* that the books to be purchased for said institution shall consist of works on science and the arts, especially such as relate to the ordinary business of life, and to the various mechanical and other improvements and discoveries which may be made."[64] But, a careful reading of the remainder of the bill clearly shows that Senator Tappen envisioned that only a small portion of the income from Smithson's bequest should be spent on the library. It is obvious that had this bill passed, the library at the Smithsonian would never have proved appealing to a professional of Jewett's stature.

However, on 8 January 1845, Rufus Choate, the bookish and articulate Senator from Massachusetts, introduced an amendment to Senator Tappen's Bill.[65] Senator Choate noted in his *Journal* on 9 December 1844 that while he was in Washington he planned to continue his reading—Thucydides, Tacitus, Juvenal, Milton, Johnson, Burke, Homer and the Bible—and then provides us with a tantalizing glimpse of his plans for the Smithsonian: "The Smithsonian Fund ought to be applied to a great library; and a report and a speech in favor of such an appropriation are the least I owe so grand and judicious a destination of a noble gift."[66]

Choate's amendment stipulated nothing less than what he had intimated in his *Journal* a month before, and he intended to achieve his objective by striking out the eighth section of Tappen's bill and substituting the following statement:

> Sec. 8. And whereas an ample and well-selected public library constitutes one of the permanent, constant, and effectual means of increasing and diffusing knowledge among men: Therefore,
>
> *Be it further enacted*, That a sum not less than $20,000 be annually expended, of the interest of the fund aforesaid, in the purchase of books and manuscripts for the formation of a library of the institution aforesaid, which, for its extent, variety, and value, shall be worthy of the donor of the said fund, and of this nation, and of the age.[67]

Senator Choate's amendment, which stirred a considerable debate in the Congress, was not presented naked, without justification or explanation; for it was prefaced by one of the most lucid and persuasive arguments in favor of libraries ever uttered by a member of the Congress of the United States. It deserves our attention, not only as a reflection of the views of a Brahmin intellectual on libraries, but as an insight into the convictions of those who desired the establishment of a great national library in the United States—a group that included Charles Coffin Jewett.

After politely reviewing Tappen's proposal, the Senator from Massachusetts turned to his own idea for the Smithsonian bequest:

> ... it has seemed to me, upon the most mature reflection, that we can not do a safer, surer, more unexceptionable thing with the income, or with a portion of the income—perhaps $20,000 a year for a few years—than to expend it in accumulating a grand and noble public library; one which, for variety, extent, and wealth, shall be, and be confessed to be, equal to any now in the world.

> ... Twenty thousand dollars a year for twenty-five years are $500,000; and $500,000 discreetly expended, not by a bibliomaniac, but by a man of sense and reading, thoroughly instructed in bibliography, would go far, very far, toward the purchase of nearly as good a library as Europe can boast.[68]

Such a library, Senator Choate noted, would be the best embodiment of Smithson's objective of increasing and diffusing knowledge among men;

> ... does not the experience of all enlightened States, does not the whole history of civilization concur to declare that a various and ample library is one of the surest, most constant, most permanent, and most economical instrumentalities to increase and diffuse knowledge?[69]

He then quoted at length from an article in the *North American Review*, lamenting the "want of large libraries" in America and comparing its inadequate libraries with the treasure houses of Europe.[70] Further, he agreed with scholars who had argued that only the federal government was capable of supporting a library of the size and nature envisioned by its advocates. But now, as if by miracle, "without the charge of one dollar on the people," the Congress could "meet the universal and urgent demand" by appropriating the Smithson bequest for this purpose.

The Senator was not unaware, however, that his suggestion might be construed by some as an attempt to "benefit a few only, not the mass; that it is exclusive and of the nature of monopoly." Such, he said, was not his intent, although it appeared obvious that not everyone would avail themselves of the library's resources. And then he anticipated a postulate that has been frequently stated by professional librarians; he argued that the many would benefit "indirectly" as a result of the new vistas open to the few—"the studious men [who] will come to learn to speak and write to and for the growing millions of a generally educated public." And in a ringing phrase he exclaimed, "No, sir; a rich and public library is no antirepublican monopoly." Senator Choate would have that fact remembered, for as far as he was concerned the new library promised to be the "Armory, the light, and fountain of liberty."[71]

And if it was to be free of charge to the public, and if it was to be freely accessible to the people–no aristocratic fiefdom for the intellectual elite–what then of the suggestion that the Library of Congress should serve the function that Senator Choate would delegate to the Smithsonian Institution?

> I answer that I think it already quite good, and improving; but that its existence constitutes no sort of argument against the formation of such a one as I recommend. In the theory of it that library is collected merely to furnish Congress and the Government with the means of doing their official business.[72]

No, Senator Choate saw the Smithsonian Institution as a much greater national resource; one that would benefit the whole nation and not just the nation's legislators.

Concluding, he asked his fellow senators if they were willing to contribute to the unfortunate situation where "there should be one drop or one morsel more of the bread or water of intellectual life tasted by the European than by the American mind. Or will you not rather say that because we are free, therefore will we add to our freedom that deep learning and that diffused culture which are its grace and its defense?"[73]

A persuasive speech indeed, and one that most of his fellows found ultimately convincing. One can only guess the overall impact of Senator Choate's address; but it is a fact that his proposal for the Smithsonian Institution–the "big library plan"–was clearly embodied in the Act "to establish the 'Smithsonian Institution,' for the increase and diffusion of knowledge among men." The act was signed into law on 30 July 1846 by President Polk.

Section eight of that act stipulated that "the said regents shall make, from the interest of said fund, an appropriation, not exceeding an average of twenty-five thousand dollars annually, for the gradual formation of a library composed of valuable works pertaining to all departments of human knowledge." Such a book budget was a librarian's dream.

Not a Bibliomaniac, But a Man
of Sense and Reading, Thoroughly Instructed
in Bibliography

The first meeting of the Smithsonian Board of Regents was convened on 7 September 1846, and an urgent order of business was to prepare a plan of organization for the Institution. Consequently, a committee was appointed to "digest a plan" and present it to the Regents at a later date. In their efforts to do so, they communicated with a number of prominent American men of science. One of those men was Joseph Henry, a Princeton professor, who at 49 years of age was considered the most prominent scientist at work in America.[74]

Professor Henry responded in detail to the Regents; and his persuasive answer, generally incorporated by the Board in the plan of organization which was adopted on 25 January 1847, set the stage for one of the most colorful episodes in the history of American librarianship—the confrontation between Henry and Jewett over the role of the Smithsonian.

When Henry responded to the Smithsonian committee, he did so in a self-confident and forceful manner that was at once convincing and reassuring to the Regents, who were groping for a way to implement the lofty ideal of Mr. Smithson now that the Institution had been established.

Briefly summarized, what Henry recommended was a careful exegesis of the founder's will; that is, the portion of the will that stated the Institution's charge as being "the increase and diffusion of knowledge among men." He argued that to increase knowledge surely meant that the Smithsonian should aid and succor scholars in their efforts to extend the boundaries of human knowledge. This, he noted, would best be achieved by providing scholars with financial support for their research.

The diffusion of knowledge to him meant the institution of an extensive publication program designed to make the latest findings of important scientific research readily available to enlightened readers everywhere.[75]

It was obvious to those reading his report that a library was not central to Professor Henry's conception of the Smithsonian's role. His appointment as Secretary by the Regents on 3 December 1846 boded ill for the "big library" advocates, although at the time few would admit the seriousness of the situation.[76]

The report of the committee charged with preparing a plan for implementing the Act of Congress establishing the Smithsonian was debated and accepted by the Board of Regents in January of 1847. This report testifies to some erosion of the strength of the "big library" advocates, but it still makes ample provision for the library when it states:

> But, without a vast accumulation of books in this metropolis, your committee conceive that the Librarian of the Smithsonian Institution may, under a proper system, become a centre of literary and bibliographical reference for our entire country. Your committee recommend that the librarian be instructed to procure catalogues, written or printed, of all important public libraries in the United States, and also, in proportion as they can be obtained, printed catalogues of the principal libraries in Europe, and the more important works on bibliography. With these beside him, he may be consulted by the scholar, the student, the author, the historian, from every section of the Union, and will be prepared to inform them whether any works they may desire to examine are to be found in the United States, and, if so, in what library; or, if in Europe only, in what country of Europe they must be sought. Informed by these catalogues, it will be easy, and your committee think desirable for those who may be charged with the selection of books, to make the Smithsonian Library chiefly a supplemental one; to purchase, for the

most part, valuable works, which are not to be found elsewhere in the Union; thus carrying out the principle to which your committee has already alluded as influencing all their recommendations, that it is expedient, as far as may be, to occupy untenanted ground.[77]

This program was further refined and, in the minds of the "big library" advocates, diluted when Henry presented his plan of organization to the Regents on 8 December 1847. The portions relating to the library clearly suggest that while Henry contemplated the establishment of a library that could serve as a national bibliographical center, he had no intention of establishing a national library in the sense advocated by Jewett and Choate:

> To carry out the plan before described, a library will be required, consisting, 1st, of a complete collection of the transactions and proceedings of all the learned societies in the world; 2d, of the more important current periodical publications, and other works necessary in preparing the periodical reports. . . .

> With reference to the collection of books, other than those mentioned above, catalogues of all the different libraries in the United States should be procured, in order that the valuable books first purchased may be such as are not to be found in the United States.

> Also catalogues of memoirs, and of books in foreign libraries, and other materials, should be collected for rendering the institution a centre of bibliographical knowledge, whence the student may be directed to any work which he may require.[78]

While Henry was steadily refining and strengthening his conception of the role of the Smithsonian, the advocates of the "big library plan" were not idle. They had selected a champion, Charles Coffin Jewett, and he had been introduced to Henry as a premier candidate for the position of "an assistant who shall be librarian" of the institution. Jewett, his friend and colleague Reuben Aldridge Guild recalled, had a reputation for "bibliographical skill and knowledge of libraries . . . [which] placed him in the front of his profession." [79]

The details of Jewett's early negotiations with Henry are somewhat unclear; but it is certain that he talked with the Secretary in 1846, and went away with serious misgivings about the future of the "big library" plan.[80] Nevertheless, somewhat later he was convinced that he should accept the position as Librarian and Assistant Secretary; perhaps the lure of a twenty thousand dollar book budget was too much for the nation's leading librarian to resist, and on 11 February 1847 Jewett agreed to accept the responsibility of building a library for the Smithsonian.

Jewett's plan, of course, was to overcome all opposition to his dream of a great national library, but he was realistic enough to realize that such a victory would not be won easily, nor immediately. Thus he accepted the compromise reflected in the plan of organization, which placed the focus on making the library a "bibliographic centre" rather than a great collection of books.

This compromise stimulated Jewett's efforts in the area of cataloging and statistical reporting—efforts that were to prove so significant to the fledgling library profession; in retrospect, the compromise might even be viewed as a blessing in disguise.

It is true, of course, that Jewett never viewed it as such in his own lifetime, and that his pugnacious and eventually irresponsible efforts to best Henry for the control of the Smithsonian finally led to his downfall. That struggle is an important part of Jewett's biography and is amply covered in several sources.[81] While it constitutes a tragic theme in any examination of his life, primary attention must fall on his great, and highly influential, successes while at the Smithsonian: (1) his *Notices of Public Libraries* (1851); (2) his contributions to cataloging practice; and (3) his influential annual reports.

*The Pioneer Attempt to Give
a Description of Our Libraries*

Joseph Henry and Charles Coffin Jewett did agree on one aspect of the library's function. Both men had great respect for the importance of bibliography to sound research, and both viewed subject bibliography as a principal means of contributing to the diffusion of knowledge.

In his *Annual Report* for 1851, Henry noted that "Every one who is desireous of enlarging the bounds of human knowledge should . . . be acquainted with what has previously been done in the same line. . . ." And then he expressed a concern that modern information scientists seem to think they invented:

> It is estimated that about twenty thousand volumes, including pamphlets, purporting to be additions to the sum of human knowledge, are published annually; and unless this mass be properly arranged, and the means furnished by which its contents may be ascertained, literature and science will be overwhelmed by their own unwieldy bulk. The pile will begin to totter under its own weight, and all the additions we may heap upon it will tend to add to the extension of the base, without increasing the elevation and dignity of the edifice.

Finally he noted that "one of the most important means of facilitating the use of libraries . . . is well-digested indexes of subjects."

In a letter, written prior to taking up his responsibilities at the Smithsonian, Jewett expressed his view on this matter, and demonstrated his own bias:

> It seems to me that the first thing to be done is to make arrangements for obtaining catalogues, printed or in manuscript, of the principal libraries of the United States; to examine these

libraries, as far as can be done personally; in order to know their general character, the statistics of their increase, & c.; and to form such alliances with the librarians as will be indispensable in making the library of the institution . . . a centre of bibliographical reference.[82]

It was in his effort to accomplish this goal that Jewett initiated a corespondence with the nation's librarians, which led in time to the publication of his famous *Notices of Public Libraries in the United States of America* (1851), hailed as "the pioneer attempt to give a description of our libraries."[83]

The significance of Jewett's "pioneer attempt" becomes apparent when one realizes that the Secretary of State of the United States, J. M. Clayton, was forced to answer a query from a British Parliamentary Commission investigating libraries in that country with the following lament:

> Department of State,
> Washington, 18 July 1850.
>
> Sir,
>
> I have the honor to acknowledge the receipt of your note of the 5th inst., in which, by instructions from your Government, you renew the request made by Mr. Crampton, under date of the 16th August last, for certain authentic information with regard to public libraries in the United States.
>
> I regret to be obliged to inform you, in reply, that soon after the receipt of Mr. Crampton's note, above referred to, an attempt was made to obtain the particular information desired, but without success; and that, with every disposition to do so, the Department finds that it has no means of gratifying the wishes of Her Majesty's Government in this respect.
>
> I avail myself, & c
> J. M. Clayton[84]

Jewett gathered the data for his *Notices* by means of a "circular letter" sent to some 900 libraries.[85] As he noted, he encountered the problem so common to modern surveys, for "many of the circulars have . . . remained to this time unanswered; others were filled up hastily, and gave but a meagre account of the collections; others, again, simply referred to some sources from which authentic details might be gathered."[86] As a result, Jewett frequently added to, or completely rewrote, the descriptions submitted.

Twentieth century librarians will find his definition of "public libraries" somewhat puzzling:

> I mean by it libraries which are accessible—either without restriction, or upon conditions with which all can easily comply—to every person who wishes to use them for their appropriate purposes. In this sense I believe it may be said that all libraries in this country,

> which are not private property, (and indeed many which are private
> property,) are public libraries.[87]

This definition demonstrates little appreciation on Jewett's part of the modern
concept of the public library, as defined by William Frederick Poole in 1876:

> ... established by state laws ... supported by local taxation and
> voluntary gifts ... managed as a public trust, and every citizen of
> the city or town which maintains it has an equal share in its
> privileges of reference and circulation.[88]

One must remember, of course, that the public library in Poole's sense was very
rare in 1849, and that Jewett's definition of "public" was quite common in his
day.[89]

His plan, he noted in the preface, was to provide a beginning in the area of
library statistical reporting, and he readily acknowledged the crudity of the
results:

> Of these libraries I have endeavored to collect such historical,
> statistical, and descriptive notices as would be of general interest;
> together with such special details as would be beneficial to those
> who are engaged in the organization and care of similar establish-
> ments.
>
> No person who will consider the vast extent of the field to be
> surveyed, the tedious process by which most of the information is to
> be collected—namely, by circular letters and private correspon-
> dence—the difficulty in this busy land of getting any one to furnish
> minute information on such subjects, the antiquated statistics, on
> these matters, which survive all other changes, in gazetteers and
> geographies, and the fact that there is nowhere in this country a full
> collection of books and pamphlets relating to the local affairs of the
> several towns and counties of the different States—no one who will
> consider these things, and remember that this is but *one* of the
> topics of inquiry to which I was required to devote my attention,
> and that, by the other duties of my office, I was prevented from
> visiting most of the libraries which I wished to describe, will be
> surprised if he should find that, in some instances, these accounts are
> not so full nor so accurate as could be desired.
>
> The publication of them, in their present state, is considered a step
> necessary to their completion and perfection. Copies will be
> distributed to librarians and others interested in these matters, and
> all persons who may receive the work are earnestly requested to
> furnish corrections, additions, and suggestions for a second edition.
> It is hoped that within a few years materials may be obtained for
> accurate accounts, embracing all historical facts of importance with
> reference to every library and every institution possessing a library in
> this country; and including the history and statistics, with a
> description of the bibliographical and scientific treasures of each.[90]

And finally, he apologized for any omissions, but the oversights, he said, could not be helped:

> Doubtless many libraries, more important than some which are mentioned in these notices, have been overlooked. The omission is unintentional. It has been utterly impossible to collect, at once, full and reliable accounts of all the libraries, small and large, in the country. This publication will make known our wish to gather all facts worthy of record respecting every one of them; and, in conformity with this plan, we would respectfully and earnestly solicit from the guardians of the libraries not mentioned here, or of which the accounts are incorrect or in any way unsatisfactory, to furnish us with the means of improving the work for a second edition.[91]

Even Jewett could not have guessed how enormously popular his *Notices* would become. Upon publication the *Notices* solicited quick and widespread response from the "guardians of libraries." Ironically, in the same report in which he announced Jewett's "separation from the Institution" Henry also pointed out that "the edition of Notices of the Public Libraries in the United States . . . is exhausted; and it will be necessary during the present year to collect the materials for a new and enlarged edition."[92] Jewett's *Notices* did much to focus professional attention on the newly organized Smithsonian Library, and contributed signficantly to making it the center of information on American libraries.

That Cherished Dream of Scholars—
A Universal Catalogue

In the conclusion of his first *Report* to Secretary Henry, Charles Coffin Jewett expressed his desire to make the Smithsonian Library, and thereby Washington, the focal point for American research, and in time to collect a library "to rank among the largest, the best selected, and the most available treasure-houses of the world."[93] But, he noted in a letter to Henry, "to lay properly the foundation of a large library is a slow work, and much time must necessarily be consumed in producing but small visible results."[94]

As far as Jewett was concerned, nothing could "compensate for the want of books," but one immediate way of establishing the library as the center of American scholarly activity would be to make it an essential reference tool for scholars:

> An important part of the plan for rendering our library immediately useful to American scholars is the proposed general catalogue of the

books contained in all our public libraries. I am not aware that such a thing has ever before been attempted on so large a scale.[95]

Jewett's plan, so revolutionary and grandiose then, will seem quite familiar to modern librarians:

> Some libraries possess printed catalogues complete nearly down to the present time; others are several years behindhand. It will be necessary to procure manuscript catalogues in continuation of those which have been printed, and to make arrangements for receiving, from month to month, or from year to year, lists of all future accessions. These supplementary catalogues should all be prepared on a uniform plan. The titles should be written on cards of the same size, so that they may be placed together in one alphabetical arrangement, in order to facilitate research. A mark placed on the back of each card will designate the library from which it came.[96]

But Jewett's quixotic plan for a national union catalog was undergoing adaptation even as he wrote, for as early as 1847, he was contemplating not just a central catalog, but rather a *printed* national union catalog, developed by means of stereotyping separate titles.

This decision set the stage for an unfolding drama that would prove both frustrating and rewarding for Jewett. For on the one hand, his plan to prepare stereotype plates made of Indiana clay—a plan Poole dubbed Jewett's "*Mud Catalogue*"—was a dismal failure; one of the most devastating of Jewett's life.[97] But, almost inadvertently, his plan for a stereotyped catalog forced him to prepare rules that would insure that descriptive cataloging was carried on in a uniform fashion. That is, so that every entry prepared in the cooperating libraries would meet the Smithsonian requirements, and would mesh nicely with the cards from other libraries; all of which would eventually constitute his national union catalog.

This desire for uniformity, expressed by every great cataloger since, led Jewett to begin a work which was eventually to appear as the second part of his *On the Construction of Catalogues of Libraries, and of a General Catalogue, and their Publication by Means of Separate, Stereotyped Titles, With Rules and Examples.* The *Rules*, which are reproduced in full in this volume, immediately became the basic guide to cataloging practice, and were not supplanted until the publication of Cutter's *Rules for a Printed Dictionary Catalogue* (1876).[98]

And so Jewett's greatest failure and greatest achievement are encompassed in one work: *On the Construction of Catalogues.* The stereotyping plan simply did not work. But, in the opinion of a recent student of the history of cataloging, the publication of Jewett's *Rules* accomplished the transfer of leadership in the field of cataloging from Europe to the United States.[99] This work is still ranked as one of a dozen or so "super-classics" in cataloging history, and led one specialist in the subject to label the period from 1850 to 1875 as the "Age of Jewett."[100]

We Have No Schools of Bibliographical
and Bibliothecal Training

What was true of the library scene in 1869, when Justin Winsor made this remark in his annual report for that year, was even more applicable in mid-nineteenth century America. How was a librarian, especially a novice librarian, to acquire the rudiments of his new profession—and once he was employed, how was he to stay abreast of new developments?[101]

Today one could turn to hundreds of books published each year on the various aspects of library and information science; and, of course, there are dozens of journals designed to meet the informational needs of library professionals. In Jewett's day none of this existed; and the librarian sought eagerly, and not infrequently without success, for the most elementary information on the administration and management of libraries.

Some few useful facts could be gleaned from articles published in literary journals such as the *North American Review*, and some information was available to librarians through the medium of Charles B. Norton's short-lived *Literary Gazette*.[102] But it was from the annual reports of America's library leaders that librarians and bookmen mined the most useful and most up-to-date information pertinent to library management.

And Jewett's annual reports, especially those issued while he was at the Smithsonian, always ranked very high on the reading lists of librarians and bookmen, both here and abroad. The reports, extensively reprinted in part two of this book, constitute some of Jewett's most important writing. Three themes dominate: (1) the need for a national library; (2) the various cataloging schemes developed at the Smithsonian; and (3) the role of libraries in a democracy.

Those themes, so central to his conception of libraries and the emerging library profession, were articulated over and over again. Reading his statement of these central ideas today, one is struck by the urgency with which Jewett makes his case, and one is reminded of the advances this profession has made since the mid-nineteenth century.

Considering the lack of library literature, the embarrassing and crippling inadequacies of American libraries, and the chaotic state of "library administration," one can easily understand why Jewett's annual reports had such wide readership and why they were so influential.[103] Today, even though many of his wildest visions are established fact, one is both inspired and provoked by his remarks.

It was the annual reports, and the many innovative projects described therein, that established Jewett as the nation's premier librarian by 1853. In that year he was to be instrumental in organizing the first meeting of professional librarians to be held in the world.

At that meeting he was lionized as America's foremost librarian and was offered a brief respite from the battleground at the Smithsonian. There, many of his most cherished dreams had fallen victim to the incessant attacks of the scientists who opposed the "big library" concept, while others collapsed, maddeningly, under their own weight.

THE LIBRARIANS' CONFERENCE OF 1853

This Is the First Convention of the Kind,
Not Only in This Country, But,
So Far as I Know, in the World

On 15 May 1853, bookmen and librarians were doubtlessly intrigued by the following notice, which appeared in Norton's *Literary Gazette*:

CALL

The undersigned, believing that the knowledge of Books, and the foundation and management of collections of them for public use, may be promoted by consultation and concert among librarians and others interested in bibliography, respectfully invite such persons to meet IN CONVENTION AT NEW YORK, ON THURSDAY, THE FIFTEENTH DAY OF SEPTEMBER, for the purpose of conferring together upon the means of advancing the prosperity and usefulness of public libraries, and for the suggestion and discussion of topics of importance to book collectors and readers.

This invitation was signed by twenty-six of the nation's leading librarians and bookmen, including Charles Folsom of the Boston Athenaeum, T. W. Harris of Harvard, Edward E. Hale of Worcester, Henry Barnard of Hartford, W. F. Poole of the Boston Mercantile Library, Lloyd P. Smith of the Philadelphia Library Company, and C. C. Jewett of Washington.[104]

The idea for the meeting appears to have been that of Charles B. Norton, a bookseller, relatively successful agent for libraries, and publisher of *Norton's Literary Gazette*, the first periodical designed specifically for the librarian. As early as the summer of 1852, Norton had proposed the idea in the *Literary Gazette*. But it was obvious to him that it was inappropriate for such a "conference of Librarians" to be sponsored by a publisher; it was essential that the meeting be endorsed by the nation's library leadership.

Once that fact was acknowledged, it was easy to agree on the person most essential to the success of the project; all concurred that the leader should be Charles Coffin Jewett, the reform and cooperation-minded Librarian at The Smithsonian. Early in 1853, Seth Hastings Grant, one of Norton's assistants, and the Librarian at the New York Mercantile Library, initiated a correspondence with Jewett designed to gain the great librarian's support for the conference idea.

Jewett's reaction to the proposal must have been heartwarming indeed, for he encouraged the conference planners in their efforts and promised his full support. In a remarkable letter to Grant, reproduced in part two of this volume, Jewett not only encouraged the promoters, but promised that "I will (Providence permitting) be present and contribute all I can."[105] He then suggested his desire to discuss his "catalogue plan, or rather the 'Smithsonian Catalogue System' " as he preferred to call it. But, most valuable of all must have been his vigorous words of assurance: "You may fall back upon me to any extent to back you up—only 'go ahead!' "

With this kind of support from Jewett, it was easy enough for the planners to bring the conference idea to fruition. And on September 15th, a number of librarians and other literary figures convened at the smaller chapel of the University of the City of New York.

As Jewett left Washington for New York, the country at large must have appeared both prosperous and tranquil.[106] But Jewett's professional life in Washington was growing increasingly complicated and frustrating, and he must have welcomed the opportunity to leave the scene of his difficulties behind for a few weeks.

Upon his arrival at the conference, Jewett found some 82 men gathered to attend the opening of the historic meeting. In his letter encouraging Grant to "go ahead," Jewett had offered a candid and revealing definition of librarians:

> The fact is our fraternity are generally very quiet, unostentatious men, not accustomed to public speaking, or fond of exhibiting themselves. Besides, our pursuits are not of such nature, as to reward our labors by brilliant discourses, or results that will resound in the busy world. We must work hard and long, with small visible effect, and in the track where hundreds, more learned than ourselves perhaps, have worked before us. More than all this, there are but few—very few—who have devoted themselves professionally to bibliography. This taken up by the young man for a few years till he can "get something better to do" or assumed as an extra labor to eke out the income of some half paid professor.

Then, almost as an afterthought he added:

> But, notwithstanding all this, there are some among us, who feel a professional interest in the office of librarian; there are private gentlemen too, engrossed in other business it is true, but still finding time for the cultivation of bibliographical pursuits with great success.

The *New York Daily Times*, which sent a reporter, described the first meeting, and in doing so, confirmed Jewett's assessment of his colleagues:

The quiet diffidence of the study seemed to have accompanied the literary treasurers, and it was some time before their proceedings took a definite form, each appearing to prefer a whispering consultation with his neighbor, to the more formal proceedings of appointing [a] President and organizing Business Committees. Ultimately, Mr. Charles Folsom, being the oldest librarian present, was requested by the delegates to open the Convention.[107]

But Folsom declined to accept the chair, and those present then turned from the oldest to the most prominent librarian among them, and unanimously elected Charles Coffin Jewett to be their President.

Upon completion of some preliminary business Jewett delivered an address to the conferees. That address, and another given on the next day, represent two of Jewett's most impressive and influential speeches; they are reproduced in full in part two of this volume.[108]

In his Presidential Address Jewett welcomed the delegates, recognizing that most of them were able to attend only upon "considerable personal sacrifice." Their purpose, he noted, was two-fold: (1) to seek "mutual instruction and encouragement in the discharge of the quiet and unostentatious labors of our vocation"; and (2) "to provide for the diffusion of knowledge of good books, and for enlarging the means of public access to them." For Jewett it was a meeting of professionals, and he insisted: "Our wishes are for the public, not for ourselves."

Reuben Guild, who helped organize the meeting, remembered that Jewett presided with "signal grace and ability," and that "his opening remarks were the keynote of the proceedings."[109]

Reading his speech today, one is struck by the way Jewett attempted to move the "literary treasurers" from a penchant to dilettantism to a truly professional stance. He urged his fellows to commit themselves to service to their countrymen, to break down barriers to the free communication of information, and to recognize the significance of books and libraries in the life of a democratic nation. Throughout he remains articulate, reasoned, and thoroughly professional. All in all it must be viewed as not only the first, but also one of the best, presidential addresses ever presented to an organization of American librarians.

While Jewett probably viewed his responsibilities on the opening day of the Conference as important, he was looking forward from the outset to the time when he could present the case for his beloved stereotype catalog plan—the plan alluded to in his letter to Grant, for as he noted in the same letter: "I want them, if they approve of it, to give me their countenance and support, for without them I can do nothing."[110] His chance came on Friday morning, the sixteenth of September. After relinquishing the chair to Mr. Haven of Worcester, Jewett launched into "an exposition in regard to the Smithsonian Institution."

And what a chance it was! For years the nation's leading librarian had been struggling in an hostile environment, enmeshed in a "warfare of words," constantly watching his program for a great national library crippled by Henry and his supporters—all determined to kill the "big library plan."

But now he stood before men who dreamed his dreams for a great national library at the Smithsonian; men who cherished books as only the scholar-librarians of that day could; and men who readily acknowledged Jewett's position at the head of his profession.

This was an opportunity not to be missed, and Charles Coffin Jewett rose eloquently to the occasion. All morning he held forth, carefully describing the history of the Smithsonian—Choate's Bill, the Compromise, and Henry's attacks on the library—and justifying that part of his address by saying:

> It has seemed to me my duty to state to you these facts, in order that you might understand the precise position of the Smithsonian Library, the ground of the expectations which had been raised respecting it, and the reasons why they had not been realized.

After stating these facts and reiterating his belief "that a large central library of reference and research will be collected at the Smithsonian Institution," he turned to a description of his catalog system, noting his intent to present "the matter fully and explicitly to this Convention." This he did, for over an hour, in full and persuasive detail. This presentation remains among Jewett's most articulate and certainly his most successful.

Jewett probably experienced the most fulfilling and rewarding moments of his professional life that morning, and he must have welcomed the frequency with which his speech was interrupted so that the sympathetic audience could express its support in the form of resolutions to the Regents of the Smithsonian.[111] First it was Elijah Hayward of Ohio moving:

> That the thanks of this Convention be presented to the Board of Regents . . . for their steady and effective efforts for the increase and diffusion of knowledge among men, and particularly for the measures which they have adopted for the encouragement and promotion of the public libraries of our country; and we have great pleasure in looking to that institution as the central establishment of the United States for the furtherance of all such objects.

Then Folsom, the Nestor of the Conference, introduced a series of resolutions endorsing Jewett's "plan for constructing catalogues of libraries"; recognizing Jewett as the inventor of the idea; and urging the continued support of the Smithsonian Regents.[112]

Finally, most gratifying of all, was Folsom's resolution endorsing Jewett's most cherished dream:

> *Resolved*, that the establishment of a great central library for reference and research, while it is demanded by the condition of the United States as to general civilization and intellectual advancement, is especially interesting to this Convention from the bearing it would have upon libraries throughout the country.

Resolved, that we deem such an establishment as being eminently worthy of support from the national treasury, and that in no way can the government better promote the progress of learning through the whole country, than by placing a central national library under the administration of the Smithsonian Institution.

But it was not to be. One wonders if Jewett, returning to Washington with spirits buoyed by his tour de force in New York, had faint and discomforting premonitions about the future. For at that moment Henry was moving to further diminish the Library's role in the Smithsonian's programs, and within a year Jewett's dreams would be crushed beyond recovery.

Nevertheless, his glory in New York was full and real, and while his dream "that this Convention may be the precursor of a permanent and highly useful association" would have to be deferred until almost a decade after his death, the Conference of 1853 deserves William Frederick Poole's label—"an era in American bibliography."[113]

TWILIGHT TIME:
THE BOSTON PUBLIC LIBRARY

A Literary Martyr to Science

In his *Annual Report* for 1854, Joseph Henry bluntly noted that "a difficulty which occurred between the librarian and myself has led to his separation from the Institution."[114] The matter-of-fact nature of his pronouncement was obviously an attempt to put behind him, quickly and quietly, the public furor provoked by Jewett's removal.

But there was really no way to diminish the outcry, for it was not Jewett's position, but rather the "big library plan," which was at stake. Reuben Aldridge Guild, Jewett's friend and biographer, put it this way:

> There was no personal hostility between the Secretary and Assistant Secretary, but the former represented science, the latter literature; and in the long controversy between the two science prevailed. . . . Gradually . . . the funds were absorbed by the scientists; the policy of the Board of Regents became less friendly to the library, and eventually Professor Jewett, tired of a warfare of words, and thoroughly disheartened, resigned his position as Librarian and Assistant Secretary.[115]

Guild, who greatly admired Jewett, overlooked the increasing animosity and disrespect that Jewett evidenced toward his superior as events rolled irreversibly toward a showdown. In a more objective assessment of Jewett's behavior, Borome concludes that in his efforts to preserve his cherished dream of a national library at the Smithsonian, Jewett took extreme measures to defeat Henry and, in doing so, committed abuses of his authority that placed him in obvious insubordination to his superior.[116] Once Jewett had advanced far beyond his defenses, Henry struck decisively, finally removing Jewett on 13 January 1855, and the Regents, thoroughly tired of the now open and embarrassing struggle, supported the Secretary against his assistant.

While there would be many broadsides exchanged between the men of "science" and the men of "literature," it was to little avail. For Jewett much was lost: his vision for a national library, his stereotyped catalogue scheme, and his ideas on a national union catalog.[117] But his reputation remained intact among the men of "literature" and it was to them that he would turn, "thoroughly disheartened," for shelter and support.

The Boston Public Library—
The Pioneer of All the Free Public
Libraries in the Country

In 1849, Jewett made the following remarks about a publishing event in American history:

> There has recently appeared from the American press, written by an American Scholar, one of the most comprehensive, profound, and elegant works which has ever been published in the department of literary history. We receive it with patriotic pride.[118]

Jewett did not identify the author by name; but everyone knew that the reference was to Boston's George Ticknor, especially when he noted that the work had been mined from the author's library "which contains some 13,000 volumes, and in the department of Spanish literature is one of the richest in the world."

It was Boston, the "Athens of America," and Ticknor, the literary and social arbiter of that great city, that offered Jewett a safe harbor in his moment of extreme frustration.

Ticknor and his fellow Brahmins had recently established a public library in Boston, one which was destined to serve, in William Frederick Poole's words, as "the pioneer of all the free public libraries in the country."[119] Throughout the nineteenth century the Boston Public Library ranked first among America's public libraries and had a considerable influence on the development of American librarianship.[120]

Scholars have repeatedly described Ticknor's class as conservative in politics, aristocratic in social affairs, and characteristically well-bred, well-educated, well-housed, and well-heeled. Clinton Rossiter presents an informal inventory of conservative principles in vogue around the middle of the nineteenth century which nicely fits Ticknor's thinking and the thinking of Boston's Brahmin class in general. They believed in the "inevitability of stratification, persistence of natural inequalities, necessity of aristocracy, importance of religion and morality, sanctity of property, unwisdom of majority rule, urgency of constitutionalism, and folly of all attempts at social and economic leveling."[121] Furthermore, Boston's "Best Men" generally agreed that Jacksonian democracy was a dangerous experiment indeed, and many aspects of American life disturbed and frightened them.[122]

Especially unsettling was the influx of rough and generally unlettered Irish immigrants into Boston in the 1840s. These immigrants were, in Ticknor's view, particularly prone to being swayed by the rhetoric of demagogues, and they were too often given to seeking violent and illegal solutions to their problems. In writing to Charles Lyell, in 1849, he described a series of riots that were then sweeping the United States, especially a recent one in New York, and noted that "nearly every person injured, killed, or arrested was a foreigner; so were three fourths of those present, and nineteen twentieths of the active mob." [23] In 1854, Ticknor noted that these same foreigners, "at no time, consisted of persons who, in general, were fitted to understand our free institutions or to be entrusted with the political power given by universal suffrage."[124]

But how was this dangerous ignorance to be eradicated, and how were these violent emotions to be channeled into productive works? Ticknor and his fellows became more and more convinced that this important task could only be accomplished by institutions that might "stabilize the Republic and keep America from being another Carthage." It was essential that they provide the means to assimilate the "masses to our national character, and bring them in willing subjection to our own institutions."[125] Such institutions should be committed to training up the members of society, "in the knowledge which will best fit them for the positions in life to which they may have been born, or any others to which they may justly aspire...."[126]

This obvious need for institutions that would contribute to the assimilation of the "dangerous classes" into the mainstream of life, coupled with the Brahmins' unmitigated faith in education and in the efficacy of the printed word in influencing and molding behavior, set the stage for the establishment of Boston's Public Library and dictated the philosophy of the public library in that city:

> (1) To educate the masses so that they would follow the "Best Men" and not demagogues; to stabilize the Republic and to keep America from becoming another Carthage.

> (2) To provide access to the world's best literature for that elite minority who would someday become leaders of the political, intellectual, and moral affairs of the nation.[127]

In 1855, shaken and embittered by the Smithsonian experience, Jewett was presented with an opportunity that would prove much to his liking. In June he left for Boston where he was employed first as a cataloger, then as the equivalent of an "acquisitions librarian," and finally, as the first Superintendent (1858) of Boston's new public library. In the latter capacity he earned $2,000 a year and enjoyed the respect due the nation's most prominent librarian.

In seeking a Superintendent, the Trustees of the Library had emphasized the fact that they wanted a man of "extensive knowledge of books, ancient and foreign languages, and of science and literature generally," and that they were well aware that such a person was not easily found, for "the general management and administration of a first class library requires an efficient and responsible head, possessing a degree of ability and qualifications, intellectual and literary, of a higher order than can be expected," from most members of the profession.[128]

Once in Boston, Jewett found himself in close contact with the country's foremost scholars and bookmen—George Ticknor, Edward Everett, and others—and he was allowed the leisure to further cultivate his already well-developed talent for organizing libraries.

Perhaps the very tranquility of the Boston years, the good relations with the Trustees, the shared social and literary beliefs, and the fact that he was never again challenged by so formidable an opponent as Henry, best explain the lack of significant writings from his pen during this period.

Readers examining the second half of this book will find nothing of Jewett's writing after his dismissal at the Smithsonian. It is true that he wrote annual reports in Boston as well as in Washington; but those in Boston rarely evidence the same excitement, the same articulate attention to grand designs such as the national library theme, or the same detailed and polemical presentations of beloved schemes such as the stereotyped catalog plan.

Outside the annual reports at Boston, he wrote little; and the only achievements that might be considered "literary" would be the two catalogs prepared under his direction and published in 1858 and 1861.[129]

Jewett was involved in a number of imaginative programs: 1) he continued to lead in the area of catalog production; 2) he pioneered in circulation-system design; and 3) he remained unrivaled among the nation's scholar-librarians, building a magnificant collection at Boston. And Jewett certainly retained his supremacy in the eyes of his colleagues, although the lack of any sort of library literature to analyze, and the paucity of Jewett manuscripts, make such matters difficult to assess.

During his later years he fell back, as do so many who were at the cutting edge of progress in their youth, and he frequently found himself being identified with the conservative position in questions relating to cataloging, Sunday opening, and circulation policies.[130]

Increasingly he immersed himself in the two great loves of his life: collection development and cataloging. By 1868, the Boston Public Library contained some 150,000 volumes and ranked second only to the Library of Congress. The Boston Public Library collections were not only large, but were also rich, containing many significant private collections including those of Nathaniel Bowditch and Thomas Prince.

And then there were the catalogs. Jewett, like every cataloger before or since, was often chided for the tedious, time-consuming, and seemingly simple-minded nature of his efforts in that area. But to Jewett the answer to such unappreciative souls came quickly and easily:

> It may, to the inexperienced, seem a light matter to turn over the leaves of a book in order to see if it be complete, to write out its title in full, to note its size, to ascertain with accuracy its authorship, to assign it a place among kindred works, to enter it in the record of accessions, as well as in the alcove catalogue, and to make from its title such references as may guide the researches of those who wish to consult it. But when this task is to be repeated a thousand times,

ten thousand times, *seventy thousand* times, the magnitude of the librarian's task will be apparent. When the difficulties are considered which he often encounters from titles inadequately representing the subject of the book, or purposely disguising it, from the inaccurate designation of authorship, or its intentional concealment, from the fact that the books are in a multitude of languages and on all subjects, that title-pages are often lost or mutilated,—not to mention many other and more troublesome problems of bibliography,—it will be perceived by any intelligent person, that such a work demands time, patience, and perseverance, far beyond those required in ordinary literary labors. But such work, however arduous, cannot be avoided in a library. A library has been defined to be "a collection of books"; but such a definition is as inadequate as to say that an army is a collection of men. To constitute an army, the men must be organized for warlike operations. So, to form a library, books and titles must be rightly ordered for their appropriate use.[131]

It is entirely possible that Charles Coffin Jewett was marshaling one of his army of books when he was struck by a fatal attack of apoplexy while working at his desk in the Boston Public Library on the afternoon of 8 January 1868.

Realizing that the end was near, Jewett pleaded to be carried home to Braintree and his wife and children. There, attended by his family and several friends, he passed away early the next morning. He was 52 years old.

There Are Some Among Us
Who Feel a Professional Interest
in the Office of Librarian

In his own day he was at the zenith of his profession; he was the man to whom most looked for leadership in library affairs; he was the first thoroughly professional of American librarians. The Boston Public Library Trustees eulogized upon their loss in the following way:

> In the death of Charles Coffin Jewett this Library is deprived of a steadfast friend, and an officer of such ingenious mind and such rare knowledge apposite to his duty, that we hardly know where to find his equal. . . .[132]

After his death his name was mentioned with respect at nearly every meeting of the American Library Association before 1900, and in 1886, William Frederick Poole made Jewett the topic of his Presidential Address, noting that:

Our profession is a debtor to Prof. Jewett for his early and scholarly services in bibliography and in library economy. . . . Indeed, he may justly be ranked as the ablest and most zealous of the early American reformers in the methods of library management.[133]

A year later Reuben Aldridge Guild recalled the "elegance of his person, the refinement of his manners, his pleasant voice, his kindly smile, his cordial affection for his friends, and his urbanity towards all," concluding that Jewett was acknowledged by all as an "honor to our profession, a model librarian. . . ."[134]

Perhaps his greatest contribution was his professionalism. He deplored the fact that so few had "devoted themselves professionally to bibliography," and he constantly worked to increase the numbers of those "who feel a professional interest in the office of librarian."[135]

Today librarians still struggle with the problems so familiar to Charles Coffin Jewett: the question of professionalism, the matter of a national library for the United States, and the problems of the acquisition and organization of library materials. One hundred years of experience and growth only prove the more how much may yet be learned from the study of a man who strived and dreamed in that dawning-time, just before the emergence of professional librarianship–The Age of Jewett.

NOTES

1. No major collection of Jewett manuscripts exists. Some few letters are scattered in various depositories, and will be cited as they prove of use. The earliest, and perhaps the most helpful sketch of Jewett is that written by Reuben Aldridge Guild, Jewett's successor at Brown, and published in the Providence *Evening Press* on 10 February 1868, two days after Jewett died. This sketch was expanded and published in the *Library Journal* 12 (1887): 507-11. Cyrus Adler, in an essay entitled "The Smithsonian Library," in George Brown Goode, ed., *The Smithsonian Institution; 1846-1896...*(Washington, 1897), pp. 274-85, presents a sketch of Jewett's life. Joseph Borome has written the most detailed and up-to-date study of Jewett's life: *Charles Coffin Jewett* (Chicago: American Library Association, 1951). There is also a sketch in the *Dictionary of American Biography*.

2. John Punchard Jewett still awaits a biographer. However, a good sketch of his life will be found in the *Dictionary of American Biography*.

3. Howard Chudacoff and Theodore C. Hirt, "Social Turmoil and Governmental Reform in Providence, 1820-1832," *Rhode Island History* 31 (1972): 31.

4. Ibid., pp. 25-26.

5. Ibid., p. 27. The Providence *Journal* noted that a despotic government would be preferable to riotous madmen who threaten "life, liberty, and property."

6. One's desire to gain insight into Jewett's social and political attitudes is frustrated by the lack of personal papers upon which to base such a judgment. It would be interesting to have concrete evidence relating to his ideas on such movements as the workingmen's movement, the anti-slavery crusade, and the anti-gallows movement. It would be difficult to imagine him being unmoved by any of these hotly contested issues in his adopted state. See Peter J. Coleman, *The Transformation of Rhode Island, 1790-1860* (Providence: Brown University Press, 1963); Marvin E. Gettleman and Noel P. Conlon, "Responses to the Rhode Island Workingmen's Reform Agitation of 1833," *Rhode Island History* 28 (1969): 75-94; Philip English Mackey, " 'The Result May be Glorious'—Anti-Gallows Movement in Rhode Island, 1832-1852," ibid. 33

(1974): 19-31; and John L. Myers, "Antislavery Agents in Rhode Island, 1835-37," ibid. 30 (1971): 20-31.

7. Wayland was the central figure at Brown, and soon came to be viewed as the leading light in Providence, and indeed, Rhode Island. See Francis Wayland and H. L. Wayland, *A Memoir of the Life and Labors of Francis Wayland*...(New York: Sheldon and Company, 1867), 2 vols., and W. G. Roelker, "Francis Wayland, A Neglected Pioneer of Higher Education," *Proceedings of the American Antiquarian Society* New Series 53 (1943): 27-78, and "Francis Wayland, 1796-1865, President of Brown University and Citizen of Providence," *Collections of the Rhode Island Historical Society* 32 (1939): 33-55.

8. Herman F. Eschenbacher, *The University of Rhode Island*... (New York: Appleton-Century Crofts, 1967), p. 4.

9. Walter C. Bronson, *The History of Brown University, 1764-1914* (Providence: Published by the University, 1914), pp. 216-17.

10. Borome, *Charles Coffin Jewett*, p. 6. A student who wished to watch his pennies, and eat at a less sumptuous table at Commons, could get by for about $100 a year in 1832-33.

11. President Wayland was disturbed by the "miscellaneous" nature of the collection, and in 1829 suggested that two avenues were open to the Trustees. First, they could use a portion of the student fees for book purchases, and second, they could establish a permanent library fund, to be raised by subscription, and use the interest from this fund for buying books. The Trustees promptly voted to use $200 of the money derived from student fees for library support, and in 1831, resolved that a library fund of $25,000 be raised by subscription, and that the money be devoted to the purchase "of books for the Library and apparatus for the philosophical and chemical departments of Brown University." Wayland, who must have recognized the optimistic nature of this undertaking, plunged vigorously into the effort to raise the prescribed sum. Almost miraculously he was able to secure some $20,000, an unheard of sum for that day; and after this sum had grown to $25,000 as a result of interest accrued, it was placed in a permanent fund, from which the library first benefited in 1839. Charles Coffin Jewett, *Preface to the Catalogue of the Library of Brown University*...(Providence, 1843), pp. 12-17. See also Bronson, *Brown University*, pp. 220-21.

12. Thomas S. Harding, *College Literary Societies: Their Contribution to Higher Education in the United States, 1815-1876* (New York: Pageant Press International, 1971), pp. 57-58. In 1833, the College Library contained 6,000 volumes and the two society libraries owned 5,600 volumes. Jewett, in his *Notices of Public Libraries*, described these libraries as follows: "These are generally valuable collections of books of a popular character. Sometimes (in Yale College particularly) they are large, well-selected, and admirably arranged and kept. Dust seldom gathers on the books in such a collection."

13. Bronson, *Brown University*, p. 147 and pp. 180-81. The Philermenian was limited to 45 members, and as a result the need was soon felt for

another literary society to serve the growing enrollment of the College. As a result, in 1806, a rival group—The United Brothers—was established. Bronson notes that, "a tincture of political controversy sharpened their rivalry, the older society inclining to the aristocratic Federals, the younger to the Republicans, the democrats of the day" (p. 181). A catalog issued by the Philermenian shows that the collection had grown to 3,224 volumes by 1849 (pp. 239-40).

14. Borome, *Charles Coffin Jewett*, p. 6.

15. J. Earl Thompson, "Abolitionism and the Theological Education at Andover," *New England Quarterly* 47 (1974): 238-61. See also Natalie Ann Naylor, "Raising a Learned Ministry: The American Education Society, 1815-1860," (doctoral dissertation, Columbia University, 1971).

16. Daniel Day Williams, *The Andover Liberals; A Study in American Theology* (New York: Columbia University Press, 1941), p. 9.

17. Ibid., p. 13. Williams notes that students were not allowed to preach sermons to their fellows unless they had first been read and approved by the faculty.

18. Thompson, "Abolitionism and the Theological Education at Andover," pp. 238-39.

19. *New York Observer* 13 (1835), No. 28.

20. Thompson, "Abolitionism and the Theological Education at Andover," pp. 253-54.

21. Ibid., p. 260.

22. Jim Ranz, *The Printed Book Catalogue in American Libraries: 1723-1900* (Chicago: American Library Association, 1964), p. 27, and Andover Theological Seminary Library, *Catalogue of the Library...* (Andover, Massachusetts: Printed by Gould & Newman, 1838).

23. Ranz, *The Printed Book Catalogue*, Chapter II.

24. Andover Theological Seminary, *Catalogue...* (1838), p. iii.

25. Harvard University Library, *A Catalogue of the Library...* (Cambridge, 1830); Ranz, *Printed Book Catalogue*, p. 27.

26. Jewett evidently was quite serious about following many of his fellow students into the foreign missionary field. But for reasons not entirely clear he did not leave the country as expected, and the library profession was spared the potential loss of one of its most distinguished members. Guild, "Memorial Sketch of Prof. Charles C. Jewett," pp. 507-508; and Borome, *Charles Coffin Jewett*, pp. 7-8.

27. Jewett described college libraries this way in his *Notices of Public Libraries in the United States* (1851): "Our colleges are mostly eleemosynary institutions. Their libraries are frequently the chance aggregations of the gifts of charity; too many of them discarded, as well nigh worthless, from the shelves of the donors. This is not true of all our college libraries; for among them are a few of the choicest and most valuable collections in the country, selected with care and competent learning, purchased with economy, and guarded with prudence, though ever available to those who wish to use them aright." For general surveys of the college library during this period see Howard Clayton, "The American College Library: 1800-1860," *Journal of Library History* 3 (1968): 120-37;

Richard Harwell, "College Libraries," *Encyclopedia of Library and Information Science* 5: 269-81 and Kenneth J. Brough, *Scholar's Workshop; Evolving Conceptions of Library Service* (Urbana: University of Illinois Press, 1953), Chapter 1. The work of Clayton and Brough is reprinted in Michael H. Harris, ed., *Reader in American Library History* (Washington: NCR, 1971).

28. For an excellent account see Marvin E. Gettleman, *The Dorr Rebellion: A Study in American Radicalism, 1833-1849* (New York: Random House, 1973).

29. Ibid., pp. xix-xx.

30. Wilson Smith, "F rancis Wayland and the Dorr War," in his *Professors and Public Ethics: Studies of Northern Moral Philosophers Before the Civil War* (Ithaca: Cornell University Press, 1956), pp. 128-46.

31. For a detailed and very informative analysis of the Conservative response, see William M. Wiecek, "Popular Sovereignty in the Dorr War— Conservative Counterblast," *Rhode Island History* 32 (1973): 34-51.

32. [Charles Coffin Jewett], *The Close of the Late Rebellion in Rhode Island; An Extract from a Letter by a Massachusetts Man Resident in Providence* (Providence: B. Cranston and Company, 1842), p. 7.

33. Ibid., p. 14.

34. Ibid., p. 2.

35. Ibid., p. 13.

36. Ibid.

37. Ibid., p. 16.

38. Life at Brown had really been disrupted by late June, when the state government requested that a "part of the College buildings" be appropriated to their use for the purpose of quartering troops. The faculty records state that the "troops were quartered in the College for several days," and that study was an impossibility. Bronson, *Brown University*, p. 254.

39. The resolution passed by the Trustees on 7 October 1841, which ordered Jewett's appointment as librarian, also stipulated that his principal responsibility was "to make out a new and approved Catalogue of the University Library. . ." Quoted in Guild, "Memorial Sketch of Prof. Charles C. Jewett," p. 508.

40. [Charles Coffin Jewett], *A Catalogue of the Library of Brown University, in Providence, Rhode Island with an Index of Subjects* (Providence, 1843).

41. Jim Ranz, *The Printed Book Catalogue*, Chapter 1.

42. Michael Harris, "Some Thoughts on the Catalog as a 'Finding List'," *Southeastern Librarian* 20 (1970): 253-54.

43. American Antiquarian Society, *Proceedings. . .*(1850), p. 14.

44. Jewett, *Catalogue of the Library of Brown University*, p. 21.

45. Ranz, *The Printed Book Catalogue*, pp. 57-58, 63.

46. Harris, "Some Thoughts on the Catalog as a 'Finding List'."

47. "[A Review of] The Catalogue of the Library of Brown University," *North American Review* 122 (January, 1844): 227-36.

48. Ibid., pp. 230, 233

49. Ibid., pp. 227-28.

50. Ibid., p. 228.

51. Guild, "Memorial Sketch of Prof. Charles Coffin Jewett," pp. 508-509; Borome, *Charles Coffin Jewett*, pp. 12-15.

52. Edward Miller, *Prince of Librarians; The Life and Times of Antonio Panizzi of The British Museum* (London: Andre Deutsch, 1967); Guild, "Memorial Sketch of . . . Jewett," p. 509.

53. Jewett's letter was written in response to a request for support for Panizzi who was having a difficult time of it in the Parliamentary investigations of his management of the Museum. However, while the letter should be viewed as a tribute to Panizzi, designed to bolster his defenses, it also appears an accurate reflection of Jewett's views. The complete letter is given in British Parliamentary Papers. *Report of The Commissioners on The Constitution and Government of The British Museum with Minutes of Evidence, 1850.* [Irish University Press, Education, British Museum vol. 3], paragraph 4293, p. 265. See also Edward Miller, *The Noble Cabinet; A History of The British Museum* (Athens, Ohio: Ohio University Press, 1974).

54. Borome, *Charles Coffin Jewett*, pp. 16-17.

55. Charles Coffin Jewett, *Facts and Considerations Relative to Duties on Books; Addressed to the Library Committee of Brown University.* Printed by Order of the Committee (Providence: John F. Moore, printer, 1846).

56. Ibid., p. 6.

57. Ibid., p. 8.

58. Ibid., p. 19.

59. Ibid., p. 21.

60. Ibid., p. 22.

61. The history of the Smithsonian is conveniently covered in Leonard Carmichael and J. C. Long, *James Smithson and the Smithsonian Story* (New York: G. P. Putnam's Sons, 1965); Geoffrey T. Hellman, *The Smithsonian; Octopus on the Mall* (Philadelphia: J. B. Lippincott Company, 1966); and Paul H. Oehser, *The Smithsonian Institution* (New York: Praeger, 1970). Hellman gives the most attention to the library. For several articles on the early years of the Smithsonian Library see George Brown Goode, ed., *The Smithsonian Institution; 1846-1896* . . . (Washington, 1897). For a very useful compilation of documents see William Jones Rhees, ed., *The Smithsonian Institution; Documents Relative to Its Origin and History, 1835-1899* . . . (Washington: Government Printing Office, 1901). Rhees' compilation reports the debates over the various proposals for the Smithsonian in full and fascinating detail. Finally, a detailed history of the Smithsonian Library, from its founding to 1855, will be found in William Dawson Johnston, *History of The Library of Congress, Vol. I, 1800-1864* (Washington: Government Printing Office, 1904), and Borome, *Charles Coffin Jewett*, deals with these years in some detail.

62. Rhees, *The Smithsonian Institution; Documents* . . . , pp. 5-6.

63. Ibid.

64. Ibid., p. 277.

65. Samuel Gilman Brown, *The Works of Rufus Choate with a Memoir of his Life* (Boston: Little, Brown, and Company, 1862), 2 vols.

66. Ibid., vol. I, p. 93. Choate, the scholar, appeared to crave his freedom from political life. His *Journal* for this period is full of his plans to "resume my courses, such as they are, of classical and elegant reading" (pp. 93-96).

67. Rhees, ed., *The Smithsonian Institution; Documents* . . ., p. 293.

68. Ibid., p. 286.

69. Ibid., p. 287.

70. The article is a review of Adrien Balbi's *Essai statistique sur les bibliothèques de Vienne* (1835); *Catalogue de la bibliothèque . . . M. le Comte de Boutourlin* (1831); and J. C. Brunet's *Manuel du libraire et de l'amateur de livres*, 3 ed. (1820), but it is primarily a polemic for a great national library for America. See *North American Review* 45 (1837): 116-49.

71. Rhees, ed., *The Smithsonian Institution, Documents . . .*, p. 292. The debate over the "big library plan" is fascinating and represents a rare glimpse of the library interests of America's most prominent politicians. J. Q. Adams, Tappen, Choate, and Robert Dale Owen, among others, spoke forcefully and articulately on the question. The debates are fully reproduced in Rhees. Owen opposed the "big library plan" viewing it "as aristocratic, designed for a few local or wealthy bibliomaniacs." See Richard William Leopold, *Robert Dale Owen; A Bibliography* (Cambridge: Harvard University Press, 1940), Chapter 14. See also Johnston, *History of the Library of Congress*, Chapter 10.

72. Rhees, *The Smithsonian Institution; Documents* . . ., p. 292.

73. Ibid., p. 293.

74. Thomas Coulson, *Joseph Henry; His Life and Work* (Princeton: Princeton University Press, 1950), p. 169. On Henry see also Paul H. Oehser, *Sons of Science; The Story of The Smithsonian Institution and Its Leaders* (New York: Henry Schuman, 1949), esp. Chapter 4.

75. Coulson, *Joseph Henry*, pp. 177-78.

76. In a letter written shortly after his appointment, Henry noted that he was determined to "prevent expenditures of a large portion of the funds . . . on a pile of bricks and mortar, filled with objects of curiosity, intended for the embellishment of Washington, and the amusement of those who visit the city. . . . The income . . . is not sufficient to carry out a fourth of the plans mentioned in the Act of Congress . . . you will readily perceive that unless the institution is started with great caution there is danger of absorbing all the income in a few objects, which in themselves may not be the best means of carrying out the designs of the Testator." Smithsonian Miscellaneous Collections, No. 356. *Memorial of Joseph Henry* (Washington, 1881), p. 409.

77. Quoted in Adler, "The Smithsonian Library," pp. 270-71.

78. "Program of Organization of the Smithsonian Institution," in the *Report of the Board of Regents of the Smithsonian Institution, January 6, 1848* . . ., p. 176. Henry's *Annual Reports* for 1847 to 1853, plus the plan of organization and other relevant documents, are all reprinted in the *Eighth*

Annual Report of The Board of Regents of the Smithsonian Institution . . .
(Washington: A. O. P. Nicholson, 1854).

79. Guild, "Memorial Sketch of Charles Coffin Jewett," p. 510.

80. Borome, *Charles Coffin Jewett*, pp. 26-27.

81. See ibid., and Johnston, *History of the Library of Congress,*
Chapter 10.

82. "Extract from a Communication of Professor Jewett . . ." in
*Report of the Board of Regents of the Smithsonian Institution, January 6,
1848. . . .*

83. *Public Libraries in the United States of America; Their History,
Condition, and Management . . . Part I* (Washington: Government Printing
Office, 1876), p. xviii and p. 759. Jesse Shera, "The Literature of American
Library History," in his *Knowing Books and Men; Knowing Computers, Too*
(Littleton, Colorado: Libraries Unlimited, 1973), pp. 128-30, deals with Jewett's
compilation and its less important predecessors. See also Borome, *Charles Coffin
Jewett*, pp. 33-36. Jewett's *Notices* was "printed by Order of Congress, As An
appendix to the Fourth Annual Report of the Board of Regents of the
Smithsonian Institution" in 1850, and then was issued with an added title page
in 1851. Most of the data was collected in 1849 and the report was transmitted
to Henry on 1 January 1850, accompanied by a letter noting that it was
"prepared in accordance with the plan of rendering the Smithsonian Institution
a centre of bibliographical knowledge."

84. The original request was not answered and so on 5 July 1850, H. L.
Bulwer addressed a note to John M. Clayton "to renew the request that was
made therein for information respecting public libraries. . . ." All three letters
are in the *Report from the Select Committee on Public Libraries . . . 1851*, p. 52
[Irish University Press, British Parliamentary Papers; Education—Public Libraries, vol. 2.]

85. The following is a copy of the circular letter: The following
questions have been prepared in order to collect as accurate statistics as possible
of the various public libraries in the United States: 1. By what name is the
library legally designated? 2. When was it founded? 3. What number of volumes
does it contain? 4. Has it collections of manuscripts, maps and charts, music,
engravings, medals, coins, etc.? If so, please to state the number of articles of
each description. 5. Are the numbers, given in reply to the last two questions,
ascertained by actually counting the volumes and articles, or are they from a
conjectural estimate? 6. What has been the yearly average number of volumes
added to the library for the last ten years? 7. What has been the yearly average
expenditure for the purchase of books? 8. Is there a permanent fund for the
increase of the library? If so, how large is it, and what sum does it yield
annually? 9. How many and what officers are employed? What are the names
and address of the present officers? 10. Has a building been erected expressly for
the library? If so, when, of what material, and at what expense? 11. What are the
dimensions, and what is the ground plan, of the library building or rooms?
12. Are the books arranged on the shelves according to subjects, or on some
other system? 13. Is there a printed catalogue of the library? If so, when was it

printed, and what is its size, and the number of pages; If more than one, what is the date of each? 14. How often is the library opened, and how long is it kept open each time? 15. Who are entitled to the use of the library, and on what terms? 16. Are books lent out to read? If so, how many are taken out annually? 17. What is the yearly average number of persons consulting the library without taking away books? 18. Have the books been injured at any time by insects? 19. Is there any regulation by which books may be lent by courtesy to persons at a distance? If so, what is it?

86. *Notices*, pp. 120-21. See also his *Second Report . . . 2 January 1850*, pp. 37-39.

87. *Notices*, p. 4.

88. William Frederick Poole, "The Organization and Management of Public Libraries," in *Public Libraries in the United States of America*, p. 477.

89. For instance, it was not all uncommon to see the library at Harvard referred to as the "public library in Cambridge." For a useful analysis of public library legislation see Jesse Shera, *Foundations of the Public Library; The Origins of the Public Library Movement in New England, 1629-1855* (Chicago: University of Chicago Press, 1949), pp. 181-99. Several acts allowing individual communities to establish libraries had been passed prior to 1849, but it was in that year that the first state public library law was passed in New Hampshire. Massachusetts followed in 1851.

90. *Notices*, p. 4.

91. Ibid.

92. 6,000 copies were printed. *Ninth Annual Report of the Board of Regents of the Smithsonian Institution . . .1855*, pp. 21, 23. William J. Rhees completed this task and published his findings as a *Manual of Public Libraries Institutions and Societies in the United States and British Provinces of North America* (Philadelphia: J. B. Lippincott & Co., 1859).

93. "Report of the Assistant Secretary Relative to the Library . . . December 18, 1848," in the *Third Annual Report of the Board of Regents of the Smithsonian Institution . . . 1848*, pp. 46-47.

94. "Extract of A Communication of Professor Jewett . . .," in the *Report of the Board of Regents of the Smithsonian Institution, January 6, 1848 . . ., p. 191.

95. "Second Report of the Assistant Secretary . . . Presented Jan. 2, 1850," in the *Fourth Annual Report of the Board of Regents of the Smithsonian Institution . . . 1849*, p. 36.

96. "Extract of a Communication of Professor Jewett . . .," p. 191.

97. William Frederick Poole, "Conference of Librarians," *Library Journal* 11 (1886): 200. Jewett's plan was to prepare a stereotype plate for each title. This plan made good sense, but unfortunately he attempted to make the plates of clay rather than metal, prompting Poole to label it "Jewett's Mud Catalogue." The clay plates warped and broke easily and simply were not suitable for the task. See Ranz, *Printed Book Catalogue in America*, pp. 47-48.

98. Borome, *Charles Coffin Jewett*, pp. 54-55, and Ranz, *The Printed Book Catalogue in America*, p. 47.

99. Donald J. Lehnus, *Milestones in Cataloging; Famous Catalogers and Their Writings, 1835-1969* (Littleton, Colorado: Libraries Unlimited, 1974), p. 64.

100. Ibid., p. 69; and Ranz, *The Printed Book Catalogue in America*, p. 35. Lehnus notes that Jewett's work was most heavily cited during the period from 1946 to 1966, almost one hundred years after its publication. He then notes that "centenarian works which are still being cited most surely deserve to be called 'superclassics' " (p. 69).

101. Most aspiring young librarians acquired their training in an apprentice-like system whereby they trained under prominent librarians like Jewett, Winsor, or William Frederick Poole. Those who could not study under these men frequently wrote asking for information. All of America's library leaders were bombarded by requests for information, and while they were committed to helping in any way they could, the pressure often became nearly unbearable. Cf. Justin Winsor, "A Word to Starters of Libraries," *Library Journal* 1 (September 1876): 1-3.

102. For an excellent study of *Norton's Literary Gazette* and the nature of library literature in general, see Donald W. Krummel, "The Library World of *Norton's Literary Gazette*," in *Books in America's Past*, ed., David Kaser (Charlottesville: University Press of Virginia, 1966), pp. 237-65. Librarians who want to get a sense of the lack of a real literature of librarianship should examine the first 28 pages of William Rhees' *Manual of Public Libraries . . . in the United States* (1859), which represent pretty much all he could pull together on the subject at the time.

103. It was Judge Joseph Story who noted that "there is not, perhaps, a single library in America sufficiently copious to have enabled Gibbon to have verified the authorities for his immortal *History* . . .," *North American Review*, 71 (1850): 185-89.

104. The Conference of 1853 is carefully analyzed in George Burwell Utley, *The Librarians' Conference of 1853; A Chapter in American Library History* (Chicago: American Library Association, 1951). See also Krummel, "The Library World of *Norton's Literary Gazette*"; Borome, *Charles Coffin Jewett*; Guild, "Memorial Sketch of Prof. Charles C. Jewett"; and Poole, "Conference of Librarians." Utley reproduces both the "Call" (pp. 16-17) and the *Proceedings* of the Conference (pp. 131-76).

105. Charles C. Jewett to S. Hastings Grant, Washington, 16 August, 1853. This letter is reproduced in Utley, *Librarians' Conference of 1853*, pp. 29-32.

106. Allen Nevins, *Ordeal of the Union, Vol. II, A House Dividing, 1852-1857* (New York: Charles Scribners, 1947), p. 77.

107. 16 December 1853. See also Utley, *The Librarians' Conference of 1853*, pp. 38ff.

108. Jewett's Presidential Address was not recorded as he delivered it, but rather was printed from a copy submitted later by Jewett. Utley, *The Librarians' Conference of 1853*, p. 40.

109. Guild, "Memorial Sketch of Prof. Charles C. Jewett," p. 510.

110. Charles C. Jewett to S. Hastings Grant, 16 August 1853. This letter is reproduced in full in part two of this volume.

111. In his annual report for 1853 he noted, "I take great pleasure in quoting the following resolutions, which were unanimously adopted, . . ." In the *Eighth Annual Report of The Board of Regents of the Smithsonian Institution* (Washington: A. O. P. Nicholson, 1854), p. 32.

112. There was some debate over who invented the scheme. See Utley, *The Librarians' Conference of 1853*, pp. 151-53.

113. Poole, "Conference of Librarians," p. 200. A number of reasons are given for the failure of librarians to organize prior to 1876: 1) Jewett's firing at the Smithsonian; 2) The financial crisis of the late '50's; and 3) The turmoil and dislocations concomitant with the Civil War and Reconstruction. Krummel, "The Library World of *Norton's Literary Gazette*," adds that Norton and Jewett lacked the perseverance and dedication that characterized later organizers like Bowker and Dewey (pp. 262-63).

114. *Ninth Annual Report of The Board of Regents of the Smithsonian Institution* (Washington: Beverly Tucker, 1855), p. 21.

115. Guild, "Memorial Sketch of Prof. Charles Coffin Jewett," p. 510. The furor over Jewett's dismissal ranks among the two or three largest ever generated by an American librarian. For various contemporary viewpoints, see the *Report* of the Special Committee . . . relative to the distribution of the income of the Smithsonian fund, in the *Eighth Annual Report of The Board of Regents of the Smithsonian Institution* (Washington: A. O. P. Nicholson, 1854), pp. 79-95, which supports Henry, and the Minority Report, written by James Meacham, which supports Jewett (ibid., pp. 247-96). Charles B. Norton tried to remain basically neutral in the matter, but tended to like the idea of the Smithsonian being a service-oriented bibliographical center and the Library of Congress being a great "national library." See Krummel, "The Library World of *Norton's Literary Gazette*," pp. 255-56. Finally, see the review of the two reports cited above in the *North American Review* 79 (October, 1854): 441-64.

116. Borome, *Charles Coffin Jewett*, p. 103.

117. In one of those curious tricks history often plays on great men, Jewett is now remembered as one of the major forces contributing to the rise of the *Library of Congress* as the national library! Secretary Henry, in his eagerness to stop Jewett's plans for the Smithsonian, increasingly supported the idea that the "national library" should be located at the Library of Congress. After Jewett's dismissal he expanded his efforts, and in 1866 he transferred the Smithsonian's 44,000-volume collection to the Library of Congress; combined with the existing collection of nearly 100,000 volumes, this made the L. C. collection the largest in the land—slightly larger than that of the Boston Public Library directed by Charles Coffin Jewett. At the same time, the new Librarian of Congress, Ainsworth Rand Spofford, utilized Jewett's arguments for a national library very effectively in his successful attempt to establish the Library of Congress in that role. See John Y. Cole, Jr., "Ainsworth Spofford and the National Library," (Ph.D. dissertation, George Washington University, 1971).

118. In the *Fourth Annual Report of the Board of Regents of the Smithsonian Institution* (Washington, 1850), pp. 32-33.

119. Poole, "Conference of Librarians," p. 200.

120. The Boston Public Library has been the subject of a number of careful studies. The earliest, and one that reproduces many documents of use to the student, is Horace G. Wadlin, *The Public Library of the City of Boston; A History* (Boston: Printed at the Library, 1911). A modern and well-written account is Walter Muir Whitehill, *Boston Public Library; A Centennial History* (Cambridge: Harvard University Press, 1956). Jesse Shera, *Foundations of the Public Library; The Origins of the Public Library Movement in New England, 1629-1855* (Chicago: University of Chicago Press, 1949), discusses the origins of the Boston Public, and reprints the famous and influential 1852 *Report* of the Trustees. For a recent and somewhat different interpretation of the origins and development of the Boston Public Library see Michael H. Harris, *The Role of the Public Library in American Life; A Speculative Essay* (Urbana: University of Illinois Graduate Library School, Occasional Paper, January 1975). This essay provides an extensive bibliography of works on public library history.

121. Clinton Rossiter, *Conservatism in America: The Thankless Persuasion*, 2d ed. (New York: Random House, 1962), p. 154.

122. A number of useful studies of Ticknor and Boston's Brahmin class exist. Especially useful is David Tyack, *George Ticknor and the Boston Brahmins* (Cambridge: Harvard University Press, 1967). Other works useful in establishing the value systems of this ruling elite can be found in Paul Goodman, "Ethics and Enterprise; The Values of a Boston Elite," *American Quarterly* 18 (1966): 437-51; Michael Katz, *The Irony of Early School Reform: Educational Innovation in Mid-Nineteenth Century Massachusetts* (Cambridge: Harvard University Press, 1968); Roger Lane, *Policing the City of Boston; 1822-1885* (Cambridge: Harvard University Press, 1967); Edward Pessen, "The Lifestyle of the Antebellum Urban Elite," *Mid-America* 55 (1973): 163-83; Robert Rich, "A 'Wilderness of Whigs': The Wealthy Men of Boston," *Journal of Social History* 4 (1971): 263-76; and Stanley K. Schultz, *The Culture Factory; Boston Public Schools, 1789-1860* (New York: Oxford University Press, 1973). A thorough study of the fear of social unrest among the Brahmins will be found in Michael H. Harris and Gerard Spiegler, "Everett, Ticknor, and the Common Man; The Fear of Societal Instability as the Motivation for the Founding of the Boston Public Library," *Libri* 24 (1974): 249-76.

123. *Life, Letters and Journals of George Ticknor*, ed. George S. Hillard, Mrs. Anna Elliot Ticknor, and Miss Anna Elliot Ticknor (Boston: James R. Osgood, 1876), vol. II: pp. 240-41.

124. Quoted in David Tyack, *George Ticknor and the Boston Brahmins*, p. 223.

125. Quoted ibid., p. 222.

126. *Report of the Trustees of the Public Library of the City of Boston, July, 1852*. City Document No. 37 (Boston, 1852), pp. 14-15.

127. Michael H. Harris, "The Purpose of the American Public Library; A Revisionist Interpretation," *Library Journal* 98 (1973): 2511.

128. Quoted in Wadlin, *The Public Library of the City of Boston . . .,* p. 63.

129. *The Catalogues* are discussed in Ranz, *The Printed Book Catalogue in America . . .,* pp. 66-70.

130. Ibid., pp. 38-39; and Borome, *Charles Coffin Jewett,* pp. 137-38, 149.

131. "Report of the Superintendent," in the *Sixth Annual Report of the Trustees of the Public Library of the City of Boston, Presented November 15, 1858.* City Document no. 46 (Boston, 1858), pp. 30-31.

132. Quoted in Whitehill, *The Boston Public Library,* p. 75. One factor that somewhat diminished Jewett's later fame was that his successor, Justin Winsor, was to become one of America's most famous and influential librarians, first at the Boston Public Library and then at Harvard. He was President of the American Library Association from 1876 to 1885, and again in 1897.

133. Poole, "Conference of Librarians," pp. 199-200.

134. Guild, "Memorial Sketch of Prof. Charles Coffin Jewett," pp. 508, 511. William I. Fletcher, a great librarian of a later era, noted that "Librarianship is not one of the recognized learned professions; in fact it is but just beginning to be acknowledged as something more than a function, for the exercise of which any fairly educated or even ordinarily intelligent person is quite competent." He further observed that "so recent is the change in this respect that most of the men are still living who by the devotion of rare talents and public-spirited zeal to this work have proved its capabilities. Their names, living or dead, constitute the honor-roll of librarianship. Among the departed, Panizzi in England, and Jewett, Lloyd Smith, and Noyes in America should be 'held in everlasting remembrance.' " Fletcher concluded that the founding fathers demonstrated that "librarianship is essentially a public service." William I. Fletcher, *Public Libraries in America* (Boston: Roberts Brothers, 1894), p. 80.

135. Jewett to Grant, 16 August 1853.

Part II

Charles Coffin Jewett
on Books, Libraries and Librarianship

THE PREFACE TO THE
BROWN UNIVERSITY LIBRARY CATALOGUE
OF 1843

When Charles Coffin Jewett joined the staff of Brown University in 1841, he did so knowing that his principal task, as defined by the Trustees, was "to make out a new and approved Catalogue of the University Library. . . ." Such a responsibility did not frighten Jewett. Indeed, he welcomed the challenge, already having had extensive experience cataloging the collection of the Philermenian Society while a student at Brown, and working on the famous Andover *Catalogue* of 1838, with Oliver A. Taylor.

The *Catalogue of the Library of Brown University*, published in 1843, was immediately hailed as a major achievement in cataloging practice. As noted earlier, Jewett's greatest advance came in his decision to prepare a two-part catalog: (1) the alphabetical list of the books in the Library, and (2) the alphabetically arranged "Index to Subjects." As Ranz points out, this advance removed the last obstacle to the eventual development of the dictionary catalog. Jewett also paid special attention to such matters as bibliographical description and the identification of authors.

Jewett prepared a lengthy preface for his *Catalogue*. Most of the material therein deals with the history of the Brown University Library and the development of the collection prior to Jewett's appointment. The final pages of the *Preface*, reprinted here, deal with the actual preparation of the *Catalogue*, and were widely read and cited by those looking for guidance in the area of catalog production.

Also included in the *Preface*, and reprinted here, are the "Powers and Duties of the Library Committee and Regulations of the Library."

• • •

Source: Charles Coffin Jewett, *A Catalogue of the Library of Brown University, in Providence, Rhode Island, with an Index of Subjects* (Providence, 1843).

The generosity of the friends of the College had furnished it with a good nucleus for a Library, and had also provided a fund for its regular and rapid increase; but, from the necessity of the case, scarcely any labor had been bestowed upon the Library for the purpose of rendering its treasures more available. It became obvious to the Committee entrusted with the care of this department, that in order to the perfect accomplishment of the object of the subscribers to the Fund, the Library must be newly arranged and catalogued. The plan of the arrangement has been selected after a wide comparison and with great deliberation. It is one, which has been fully tried, and has met the entire approbation of eminent librarians. It is simple and convenient, and admits of indefinite extension.

Shelves for the accommodation of thirty thousand volumes have been constructed, with every reference to neatness of appearance and economy of room. The books have been assorted, according to their sizes, and as far as convenient according to their subjects, and placed permanently upon the shelves. A minute classification of the books according to the subjects of which they treat has not been thought desirable, because it has been found impossible to continue such a classification, in a library receiving constant accessions, without the sacrifice of more important advantages. In fact, the value of such an arrangement is very trifling, provided the Catalogue be properly constructed. The shelves are numbered, and the books are numbered in their order upon the shelves. The number of the shelf and the number, denoting the place of the book upon the shelf are, or should be, both stamped upon the back of the book, to promote facility of reference. Both these numbers are expressed in the Catalogue.

The Catalogue consists of two parts: a descriptive Catalogue of all the works, which the Library contains, and an Index of Subjects.

In the descriptive Catalogue,* the works are placed in alphabetical order under the names of their authors, and the names themselves are alphabetically arranged. The complete works of an author are, however, placed first under his name, and biographies, by another hand, last, unless they have been previously noticed in connection with some other article. A few other variations from the alphabetical arrangement have, for obvious reasons, been admitted. Anonymous works, of which I have been unable to ascertain the authors, are placed under the most important word of the title, or under the subject to which they relate. In some cases I have grouped a considerable number of these together, under a title to which they indirectly relate, e.g. under Great Britain, United States, etc. In some instances, also, anonymous works, which relate to particular persons, or their writings, are put under the names of those persons. So much of the title has in every case been given, as seemed necessary to designate the work. The

---

*In the arrangement of the Catalogue I have followed the plan of Mr. O. A. Taylor's Catalogue of the Library of the Theological Seminary in Andover, Mass., a work far superior to all others of the kind, which have been published in this country, and which has been pronounced in Germany a model for a Catalogue. I have found my own labors considerably abridged by the use of this accurate work.

phraseology and the orthography of the titles, sometimes quaint and awkward, have been scrupulously retained. As the book has been passing through the press I have added biographical notices of authors, so far as my time would allow. These extend to most cases where they were necessary to distinguish between two or more authors of the same name; to all ancient writers; and, in the last half of the book, to nearly all American writers. So far as they go, they will I hope be found convenient. I have also occasionally added bibliographical notes. I have felt obliged to limit myself more narrowly, than I could have wished, in reference both to biographical and bibliographical notices, in order to avoid increasing too much the size of the volume, or delaying too long its publication.

The Index of Subjects, I have endeavored to arrange in such a manner as to answer the purpose of an alphabetical index, and as far as possible of a classed index. There is certainly room for a great variety of opinion as to the best method of constructing such a work. I cannot but think, however, that the one here offered will be found more convenient to the class of persons, who will use this Library, than if it had been arranged according to any of the bibliographical systems, which have been proposed. The plan is in most respects like that of the Signet Library Catalogue, of Edinburgh, a work which has been highly commended in England.

I have made the Index as minute and full, as the circumstances of its preparation seemed to warrant. To refer, under each subject, to every book in the Library, in which it is discussed, would be the labor of years, rather than of a few weeks; and would require a volume larger than the Catalogue itself. I have entirely excluded from the Index several large classes of works; because the insertion of them, it is believed, would have increased the size of the volume, without proportionally increasing its value; e.g. all miscellaneous Sermons, many religious works, which it is difficult to refer to any particular topic, and many of those 'cruces bibliographûm,' usually placed under the head of Miscellanies.

Of the labor which this work,* easy of execution as to some it may appear, has cost me, I shall say but little. None will appreciate it but those who have been engaged in similar labors, and they will estimate it aright, without any remarks of mine.

A more minute detail of the principles upon which the Catalogue and the Index are constructed is deemed unnecessary, inasmuch as they can be more readily learned from an examination of the book, than from the longest description.

I have aimed at accuracy. If, in a work, so abounding in details, I have not avoided all errors, I am confident that those who are best acquainted with such labors, will be the last to censure me. I have relied upon the best bibliographical

---

*Ebert, in his "Bildung des Bibliothekars," gives the qualifications of a German librarian. Few, however, it is believed, have ever engaged in the work of arranging and cataloguing even the comparatively small library of a New England college, without being painfully impressed with the importance of all the varied learning which he describes. Some of the difficulties which attend the preparation of a Catalogue are very happily illustrated, in an article, on Libraries and Catalogues, in the London Quarterly Review for May, 1843.

authorities in my reach. To avoid misleading others, I have, in most cases, when I have placed books published anonymously under the names of the authors to whom they are attributed, included the title in brackets.

All important errors which have been discovered are noticed at the end of the Catalogue.

• • •

Charles C. Jewett, Librarian

Brown University
Providence, R.I., Aug. 12, 1843

POWERS AND DUTIES

of

THE LIBRARY COMMITTEE

and

REGULATIONS OF THE LIBRARY.

LIBRARY COMMITTEE

1. The Library shall be under the immediate direction of a Joint Committee of the Corporation and Faculty of the University. This Committee shall be entitled, "the Joint Library Committee," and shall consist of not less than six, to be chosen annually, three by the Corporation, and three by the Faculty.

2. It being required by one of the conditions of the subcription to the Library Fund, that the selection of books for the Library and of apparatus for the Philosophical and Chemical Departments shall be made by a Joint Committee of the Corporation and Faculty, it is hereby made the duty of the Joint Library Committee to make the purchase of apparatus for said Departments, and likewise of books for the Library; to advise and direct the Librarian in the discharge of the duties of his office; and to regulate and conduct

all the concerns of the Library, not otherwise provided for by the Corporation. They shall hold regular meetings, at least once in every term of three months; keep a record of their proceedings; and shall present to the Corporation, yearly, a detailed Report of the actual state of the Library; of all expenditures for books and for apparatus; and of all other matters confided to their direction and supervision.

LIBRARIAN

3. A Librarian shall be annually appointed. It shall be his duty to take good care of all the books and other property belonging to the Library; to arrange in proper order all books, pamphlets, charts, etc.; and, under the direction of the Joint Library Committee, to make a full and accurate catalogue of the same. He shall record all fines incurred by a violation of the regulations of the Library; and, at the close of each term, shall furnish the Register with a list of the same, who shall collect them with the regular term bills. He shall carefully examine the whole Library, under the direction of the Library Committee, at least once in every year; and he shall present to said Committee a circumstantial report, in writing, of the results of such examination. He shall, moreover, perform such other duties, appertaining to his office, as the Corporation or the Library Committee may, from time to time, prescribe.

GENERAL REGULATIONS

4. The Library, in term time, shall be open for using books, not less than one hour a day on the first five secular days of the week, except on the days of Public Fast and Thanksgiving, on the 4th of July, and on such other days as, from special reasons, the Library Committee shall direct it to be closed. During Vacations, the Library shall be open not less than once a week, at such time as the Library Committee shall prescribe; and the same Committee are authorized, whenever they shall see fit, to increase the time for which the Library is required to be open during term time.

5. The members of the Corporation, the President, Professors, Tutors, and Register; all resident Graduates; all the Donors to the Library fund; all Donors to the fund for building Rhode Island Hall; and all Donors to the Library to the amount of $40, residing in the city of Providence, shall be entitled to the use of the Library, without expense. The Undergraduates shall also be entitled to the use of the Library, and shall be charged therefor the sum of one dollar per term.

6. The privilege of reading or of consulting books in the Library, under such restrictions as the Library Committee may prescribe, shall be extended to all graduates of the University; to all settled clergymen of every denomination residing in the City of Providence and its vicinity; and to all other persons on

whom, for the purpose of advancing the Arts, Science or Literature, the Corporation or Library Committee may, from time to time, confer it.

7. No book shall be borrowed from the Library or returned to it, without the knowledge and presence of the Librarian or his Assistant, who shall take particular notice of the state of each book, when delivered out, and when returned. And every book, when lent, shall, if the Librarian so direct, have a paper cover on it, which shall be returned undefaced with the book. And the Librarian shall require of the borrower a receipt for every book, if he be present; otherwise the book may be delivered on his written application. In no case, however, shall books be lent to Undergraduates, unless they are present to sign a receipt for the same.

8. No person except officers of instruction shall borrow from the Library more than one folio, which he may keep four weeks; or one quarto, which he may keep three weeks; or two octavos or two duodecimos, which he may keep two weeks.

9. For every book not returned at the time specified, the person borrowing it shall pay for each folio or quarto, three cents; and for each octavo or duodecimo, two cents, for every day, until it shall be returned.

10. The officers of Instruction shall not, without the permission of the Library Committee, be allowed to borrow more than ten volumes at any one time—the loan may be renewed to them if required.

11. All the books, whether in possession of undergraduates, resident graduates, officers of instruction, members of the corporation, or others, shall be returned to the Library, on or before the Friday preceding the close of each collegiate term. Any person who may fail to comply with this requirement, shall pay twenty-five cents for each volume of which he retains possession.

12. If any book borrowed from the Library be injured or defaced by writing in it or otherwise, or be lost, the Librarian shall make immediate report of it to the Library Committee. And if the borrower be a graduate or undergraduate, the Library Committee shall oblige him to replace it as soon as possible, with one of equal value; or they may punish him by fine or otherwise; and if such volume be part of a set, the borrower shall be obliged to replace the whole set, or be punished, as above; and until this be done, he shall not be allowed to borrow any other book.

13. No book can be renewed to any undergraduate or resident graduate, unless it be brought to the Library.

14. No Undergraduate, while receiving books, shall take down any book from the shelves without special permission from the Librarian.

15. No person shall lend to any other a book which he has borrowed from the Library, nor let it go from under his personal custody. And no book shall, by any person, be carried out of the City of Providence, without the special permission of the Corporation or of the Library Committee.

16. Inasmuch as the Librarian is held specially responsible for the safe keeping of the books, etc., belonging to the Library, no person shall be allowed to enter the Library, unaccompanied by him or by his authorized agent.

17. If any Undergraduate desires to borrow a book, which is lent out of the Library, he may leave his name and the title of the book with the Librarian; and when the book shall be returned, the Librarian shall reserve it for the person so applying; provided he call for it at his next time of receiving books from the Library.

18. Such books, maps, charts, etc., as have been, or which may be presented, with the intention or request that they shall not be lent from the Library, shall in no case be lent therefrom. Books, which are valuable for their plates, or for their rarity or antiquity, and all others which the Library Committee may designate as works of reference, shall not be lent; but may be freely consulted in the Library.

19. The privileges of the Library shall be withdrawn from all such persons as may incur fines under the preceding Regulations, until such fines shall have been paid. And the Librarian is authorized to suspend or to withdraw the privilege of borrowing books from the Library, or of reading books therein, from any person who may wilfully violate any of its regulations.

20. The Joint Library Committee are authorized to establish, from time to time, such additional regulations, not incompatible with the laws of the University, as shall be found proper and necessary, for the safety of the Library and the due administration of its concerns. All such additional regulations shall, however, be reported to the Corporation.

The above Regulations of the Library were established by a vote of the Corporation of Brown University, at their Annual Meeting, Sept. 2, 1841.

FACTS AND CONSIDERATIONS
RELATIVE TO DUTIES ON BOOKS

Shortly after returning to America from his triumphant book-buying tour of Europe in 1843-45, Jewett wrote one of his most articulate and persuasive essays. This effort was stimulated by the new tariff law—the Walker Tariff—that had been proposed and that, if passed, would have substantially increased the tax on books imported into the United States. Jewett expressed a view that is now quite acceptable when he noted that, while such tariffs might serve the special interests of publishers and authors, they also had the potential for significantly limiting the number of books—and thereby the amount of information—available to the citizens of the United States. Such a situation was intolerable in a democratic republic where the people must be wise to govern well.

His lengthy essay, reprinted here, was a persuasive attempt to counter the pro-tariff argument. In addition to being a spirited argument in favor of freedom of access to books and information, the essay contains much interesting information on the American book trade, and testifies to the extent of our dependence on the European publishers and book trade for most of the books and magazines acquired by American libraries. Jewett's essay did not achieve its purpose, since the Walker Tariff was passed in 1846.

• • •

The Secretary of the Treasury proposes to place a duty of 20 per cent. ad valorem, on all books imported;— that is, he, in effect, proposes to increase the duty 7,26 per cent. on all books subject to duty, by the present tariff, and to impose a duty of 20 per cent on a large class of books, which by the present tariff are admitted, duty free.

• • •

Source: Charles Coffin Jewett, *Facts and Considerations Relative to Duties on Books; Addressed to the Library Committee of Brown University* (Providence: John F. Moore, Printer, 1846).

This great increase of duties will fall heaviest upon books printed in Latin, Greek, Hebrew, and living foreign languages; on polyglots, lexicons, and dictionaries; on reports of legislative committees, and on old English books. Now these books are purchased more than the remaining class by mechanics, students, clergymen, &c.—men more than most others deserving of special favor from the government,—the two latter classes proverbially poor and notoriously ill requited for their toil and sacrifices. The only class of books upon which the proposed tariff diminishes the duty, consists of new English books, bound, a class purchased more than any other by the rich.*

Besides this, the proposed tariff imposes a new and oppressive duty of 20 per cent. upon all books imported for seminaries of education, &c., which seminaries are supported for the most part by charity, and whose only object is to advance the interests of science and literature, and promote the general diffusion of useful knowledge. During the year before last, several public spirited individuals, in the city of Providence, subscribed the sum of five thousand dollars, to purchase foreign books for the Library of Brown University. Had the proposed tariff been in force when these books were imported, we should have received but four-fifths of the intended gift, while the remaining fifth would have been bestowed upon the government of the United States!

It would appear that the duty on books recommended by the Secretary, could only have been proposed for the purpose of augmenting the revenue from this source; unless, as is possibly the fact, it occurred through inadvertence.

Now, if the quantity of books imported should continue to be the same as during the last year, the revenue would be increased by 20 per cent duty. But, it must be obvious to any one at all familiar with the subject, that the number of books imported would be greatly diminished. Indeed, so onerous would the duties be, that they would be quite prohibitory . . . It should be remembered that there is a radical difference betwen the demand for books, or of food for the mind, and of food for the body. The latter cannot be dispensed with, and the demand for it will be comparatively constant, even though high duties be imposed upon it. The former, however, can be dispensed with, and the demand will diminish as the taxes increase.

But, even if the amount of revenue from books, should continue the same, or should it even be doubled, it would still constitute a very small item in the $22,500,000 to be collected annually at the Custom Houses; for, be it noticed, the whole amount of money raised during the last year by duties on books, was only $29,210,87. It is not the amount of money raised that we complain of, so much as the influence of raising it in this way. It is not simply paying more money for the books which we buy, but excluding a large number which, without a tariff, would be imported, and which we believe would subserve the best interests of the community.

---

*The proposed tariff diminishes by 1.44 per cent the duty on books printed in other languages than Hebrew, Greek, Latin or English, when in sheets or pamphlets. On the same books, however, when bound, it increases the duty by 13,08 per cent.

Further; ad valorem duties on books are the most unequal and oppressive that can be made.

In this respect, books differ widely from all other classes of merchandize. All ad valorem duties, afford facilities for defrauding the revenue by false invoices; but, in other articles, it is not so impossible to guard against fraud. They have a market value, readily ascertainable. They are quoted in the prices current. On the contrary, it is but comparatively a small number of books, which can be said to have any fixed market value. They are not and never can be quoted in the prices current. The price of a book, which has been published two or three years, is extremely fluctuating and capricious; equally good copies of the same work being frequently to be had in some shops for a half, a third part, and sometimes even for a twentieth part of the least which they can be bought for in other book shops, in the same street. Now, I say, that *no custom house officer, no bookseller even, in the United States, is competent to decide respecting one half of the books imported into the United States whether they are invoiced honestly or not.* A man who has no conscience about defrauding the revenue, might pass books at the custom house for one-eighth of one per cent. on their real value, while an honest man might be compelled to pay in duties six times the price which he paid for the book.

That I am not exaggerating will be rendered manifest by a few examples.

I recently saw an edition of Homer, in one volume, folio, (Editio princeps, Florence, 1488,) sold at the Blackstone sale, in London, for fifty-eight and a half guineas, (about two hundred and ninety-two dollars.) It was only decently bound, and materially speaking, of no great value. If such a book were invoiced at two dollars, probably no custom house officer in the United States would have his suspicions awakened by it. Thus one man might pass the book for forty cents duty, while another would be compelled to pay fifty-eight dollars!! The case would be much stronger if we take such a book as the first edition of Shakspeare, (one vol. 1623,) one copy, at least, of which, costing six hundred dollars, has been imported into the United States. The book has sometimes been sold for one thousand dollars. But how many custom house officers, how many booksellers even, in the United States, know whether the book be worth ten dollars or a thousand?

I bought, in Leipsic, a set of the *Allgemeine Deutsche Bibliothek,* (a valuable work for a public library,) in 139 decently bound octavo volumes, with numerous plates, for the small sum of four dollars. If this book were invoiced fairly, who could blame a custom house officer for suspecting an attempt to defraud the revenue? But how can he ascertain the value of the work? All he can do is to appeal to a bookseller. But perhaps there is not one bookseller in the city of New York, who ever saw or heard of this work, or of 2,500,000 more, out of the 3,000,000 books which have been printed, almost any one of which is liable, at any time, to be presented at the custom house. A bookseller, when thus appealed to, could do nothing more than to refer to his catalogues for information. But the price of the work cited above, (for which I gave four dollars,) is stated in recent German Catalogues, (say Engelmann's, 1837,) to be 145 dollars! I might thus be compelled to pay 28 dollars in duties on a work, which I actually bought for four dollars! The very possibility of such an occurrence, is sufficient to show the unequal operation of such a duty; but, in point of fact, such occurrences would not be mere possibilities. They would not be mere exceptions to the common rule. They would be occurring, in a more or less aggravated form, *every day*. They would be offering a premium upon fraud. They would render it the height of honest stupidity to invoice fairly what are called rare books; a class of books at present much purchased by Americans, and one, the importation of which, should by all means be encouraged. They would render it impossible for our literary institutions to avail themselves of the frequent opportunities, which occur at the book-auctions of Europe, to procure for our public libraries, at a trifling price, the literary treasures of other nations and past ages. And, further, they would render it impossible for a conscientious importer of books to live by his business, so long as less scrupulous men are engaged in the same trade.

Thus far I have endeavored to show, that the proposed change in the tariff on books, would operate to the disadvantage of those classes of consumers who are most entitled to favor; that it would impose an unreasonable and oppressive tax upon our public institutions of learning; that, instead of increasing, it would diminish the revenue, inasmuch as it would be quite prohibitory of old books and of books in foreign languages; and finally, that ad valorem duties on books must necessarily be, in practice, unjust, and injurious to the best interests of the community.

I proceed now to consider the question, how far, upon enlightened principles of public policy, any duties on books can be justified.

It seems to me that (protection to our own publishers, authors, &c. apart,) imperative reasons exist for placing books among articles free from all duty. "Books," says Sir H. Parnell,* "may be truly called the raw materials of every kind of science, and art, and of all social improvement." The raw material should not, most certainly, be subjected to heavy duties.

We recognize the importance of education; but students cannot be educated without books, and many of the books needed, are not, and cannot be produced in this country. We recognize, too, the importance of what are commonly termed the learned professions; but the members of these professions depend mainly upon foreign books. It is necessary that we should have accomplished architects for the erection of our public and private edifices, and skilful engineers for conducting our works of internal improvement; but these men must get their knowledge mainly from foreign books. If they are restricted to American books, they will be continually led into errors, which would injure us in our reputation, and diminish the value of our investments. Our mechanics, too, are many of them dependent upon foreign books. American mechanics possess a peculiar skill in applying scientific discoveries to practical purposes. How many millions of dollars have been saved for us by such applications, and how many millions more have been gained. Now these discoveries are most of

---

*On Financial Reform, 3d Ed. p. 30.

them detailed in foreign books, and in the journals of foreign scientific societies, most of which are not and cannot be reprinted here. If we prohibit or render dearer the books which these men need, we do an incalculable injury to the whole community. If to gain a revenue of thirty thousand dollars, we deprive a Fulton of the very book that would suggest to him the new application of some scientific principle, destined to change the whole face of society, and increase incalculably our wealth, is it a wise policy which we pursue?

But, it will be said, the repeal of duties on books would ruin our own authors and publishers, and consequently all who are dependent upon them. I will first consider the effect of a free admission of all books upon *American authors.*

The admission of books, in all other languages than English, would not of course affect our authors, in any degree, unfavorably. On the contrary, it would be of great benefit to them. It would furnish them at a cheaper rate with the tools with which they must work. Nor can the free admission of English books be prejudicial to the interests of American authors, except such of them as deserve no encouragement; for, a "book which is a book," will in America always find a publisher and be well paid for, with or without a tariff. Our authors will have more to do without a tariff than with one. Do our authors desire a tariff to protect them? I believe not. I have never heard them as a body, or as individuals, demanding high duties, or any duties on books. They do not need or desire such duties. On the contrary, I have always found them advocating the admission of books duty free.

I proceed to consider the effect of abolishing the duties on books upon *American publishers.*

We would not, of course, wish to urge the adoption of a policy which would injure or dishearten American publishers. On the contrary, we would in all proper ways encourage and protect them. Their republications of English books are scattered broadcast over the whole land, with a degree of enterprise which has never been approached and which defies rivalry. They are disseminated all over the south; they penetrate to the remotest settlements of the west, and are to be found in the log cabins on the outposts of civilization. I have seen them at a greater distance, in the bookshops of Leipsic, and in the small library of the rude but hospitable inn, on the top of the Grimsel. Wherever they go, they carry with them (some of them at least) a humanizing and enlightening influence. We repeat, it is not our wish to stop all this. If a tariff be necessary to protect this branch of industry, we will accept the tariff, not only without complaint, but cheerfully; with this proviso, however, *that the tariff be restricted to the articles upon which protection is needed;* in other words, *that the duties be laid upon books which have actually been reprinted, or which some publisher pledges himself to reprint, and only upon these.* No one would, we presume, object to such a tariff. It would place a duty of 20 per cent, more or less, upon some 200 English books, annually. But it would leave free all other English books, and all books in other languages. The number of new works annually published in Great Britain is about 2500. With a tariff upon such of these as are reprinted, and upon no others, we should have 2300 of these (or all we want of them) duty free. The 7000 different works issuing each year from the German press, and the 6000 from the French press, and those published in all other countries, as well as all the 3,000,000 which have been published since the invention of printing, would be admitted duty free. For upon all of these, no reasonable plea whatever, can be urged for a tariff. No one would be injured by admitting them duty free. On the contrary, everybody would be benefitted.

The English book-trade remaining in its present position, however, the American publisher certainly needs no tariff to protect him.

The fact, at present, is, that the American republisher, with a tariff equal on English books to about 20 per cent., can undersell the English publisher by at least 80 per cent. I have compared on the New York trade sale catalogue, for the present year, the prices of 180 reprints, with the prices of the cheapest English editions of the same works. I included in the number several works which have been much enlarged and improved by the American editors, and which are consequently much better books than the originals. These books command prices as high as the originals, and sometimes higher. I rejected most of the cheap republications of novels, although the difference between the prices of the English and American editions is much greater with respect to those books than to any others. The average price of the American editions of 180 works thus selected, was ascertained to be only one-third that of the English editions, the 20 per cent. tariff not being taken into the account. It is not, probably, too much to assert, that American reprints of English works cost on an average, per copy, not more than one-sixth of the original editions.

The advantages which the American republisher has over the English publisher, and which enable him to furnish his books at a price so much lower, are as follows:*

1. The American publisher has no copyright to pay. This is already a great gain.

2. The American publisher is exempted from the taxes' which are so oppressive to the English publisher. These taxes have recently been much diminished, but they are still very heavy. They consist of the duty on paper, the

---

*It may be well to state here the fact, that the mere price of printing (i.e. composition and press-work) is as cheap in America, as in England. In England the price for composition is calculated on the 1000 letters (the average of the letters being considered the en quadrat.) In America it is counted by em quadrats.

The English price for 2000 letters (1000 ems) of any type between English and and Brevier, is regulated at 1 shilling.

Press-work per 500 sheets, averages 3 shillings and 8 pence. These are the prices *uniformly* paid.

five copies of all works to be given to certain public libraries, and the duty on advertisements.*

It is very true, that the drawback on all books exported, partly counterbalances the excise; but not wholly, and in the actual state of the trade, (and it is only that of which I speak at present,) this drawback in most cases goes not to the publisher, but to the exporter of the books.

3. Another advantage which the American publisher has over the English publisher, is that the taste of the English reading public demands a more elegant and expensive book. The reading community in England is much smaller than in America. It is much richer, and consequently able to pay more. The taste has been formed for elegant printing. A style of execution which would be quite satisfactory in America, would condemn a book to neglect and oblivion in England. No one can appreciate the full force of this consideration, unless he has observed the facts bearing upon it, in both countries. But any one familiar with these facts knows that it is at present utterly impossible to command the market of both countries with one edition of any popular work.

4. Another advantage that the American republisher has over the English publisher, is that the former incurs a much lighter risk than the latter. The most sagacious publishers are, every day, deceived in their anticipations of the success of new works. The risks to which I refer are not such as are common to all business transactions; they are altogether peculiar. The calculation of these risks is exceedingly difficult, and is the great element which secures success, or occasions failure to every publisher. There is this peculiarity about them, that the caprices of men are to be taken into account much more than in any other business. He is a rare man who can judge of the success of any considerable number of books of which he only sees the manuscript. The man does not live, who can calculate with safety the chances of success for two hundred books a year, in a market three thousand miles from his home. Now all this risk is reduced to comparatively nothing for the American publisher. He takes the book when it has been tried and approved, or at least, when it has been printed, and he can subject it to the judgment of several impartial and competent "readers."

---

*To show the operation of these duties on publishers, I extract from McCulloch's Dictionary of Commerce, the following estimate of the cost of a volume of 500 pages 8vo. with the ordinary quantity of matter on a page, and sold by retail at 12 shillings per volume; showing what portion of the cost consists of duty, and the profits of the author and publisher on each edition of 750 copies, when all is sold off.

	Total cost.			Whereof duty.		
	£	s.	d.	£	s.	d.
Printing and Corrections	95	4	0	0	0	0
Paper	48	0	0	7	4	0
Boarding in Cloth	24	0	0	1	3	3
Advertising	50	0	0	12	10	0
	217	4	0	20	17	3

5. The American publisher can count on a much larger sale than the English. Consequently he can afford to sell his edition much cheaper.

All these advantages and others of less importance, the American republisher at present enjoys over the English publisher.

But, it may be argued, "without a tariff, additional copies may be printed for our market from the first editions, much below the cost of those editions at home, in fact, for the bare cost of paper, press-work and copyright, and in case a second edition of the book be called for in England, it may be stereotyped, and thus the English publisher be enabled to undersell permanently the American republisher." I believe I have stated the argument in its full force.

Now it is obvious, that in respect to a second edition, the American re-publisher has nothing to fear from the English publisher. He has exemption from copyright, a superior knowledge, and a better command of the market, diminished risks and time, all in his favor. That with these he could successfully compete with the English publisher, no one acquainted with the publishing business in both countries can doubt.

All that the American publisher has to fear, then, is from the first edition. The English publisher may, it is said, print off extra copies on cheap paper, and send them over to this country, or he may stereotype the book in the first edition and thus control the market.

Now, with reference to extra copies from first editions, it is probable, that if extra copies (say two hundred and fifty) of every book published in England were struck off and sent over here, a great loss would accrue to the publishers. Scarcely one half of these books ever pay for themselves at home, and not one out of five ever reaches a second edition, and not one out of ten has been thought worthy of a reprint in America. Very few books are stereotyped in England, in the first edition; fewer by far than in America. If English publishers should stereotype their books, with a view to supply the American market, they would be likely to lose money, unless they could judge as well before a book is printed of its probable success in America, as American publishers have been able to do with reference to other books, after they had been printed and circulated in England. Every book, or nearly every book, is ushered into the world with the strongest hopes of success on the part of its publisher; yet, as I have already remarked, nearly one half of the books published in England prove failures. How then can selections be made? It may possibly be said that American importers would order the books in advance. But how can American importers know the merits of a book which they have never seen? In case of a few works, by distinguished and popular authors, this can be safely done, and is done even now. But this could be done safely with but very few works. And again, in few cases is it probable that more than two hundred and fifty copies would be struck off from the first edition for the American market; but for all books worth reprinting, even five hundred copies would not be a hindrance to the American publisher. So large is our market for really popular books, (and only such do we now republish,) that five hundred copies would only be an advertisement.

From all this it appears probable that additional copies of *some works* would be printed off from the first edition, for the American market; that some *few* books would be stereotyped in the first edition with the hope of supplying the American market; and that more would be done, than at present, in both these ways. But that enough *could* be done to render protection necessary, in order to enable American publishers to reprint all popular English works, it seems to me no one can suppose, who considers attentively the foregoing remarks, or who will weigh carefully the following facts.

1. In Belgium for several years past the republication of French copyright books has been carried on to a vast extent, and no efforts of the French publishers have been able to prevent it. Now the difference in price between the Belgian reprints and the French originals is much less than between the American reprints and the English editions. Belgium is separated from France only by an imaginary line, while America is three thousand miles and more distant from England. The Belgian tariff on books is less than three per cent. The only advantage which the Belgian publisher has over the French publisher is an exemption from copyright, and the diminished risk arising from his taking the book when it has passed the ordeal of one edition.

2. For several years past the republication of English books has been carried on to a considerable extent in Germany, and the publishers have grown rich in the business. No tariff on books exists in Germany.

3. It is notorious that nothing but a copyright can protect publishers from rival editions of popular works, even in their own country, because all very popular works will support two or even more editions, of different prices and styles of execution, when thrown simultaneously upon the market. An international copyright law is the only thing which could break down our publishers.

But although these facts and considerations are to my mind conclusive in showing that the American republisher has nothing to fear from the repeal of duties on books, still I close the discussion as I commenced it, by saying that if others should come to a different conclusion, no one probably would object to a tariff so framed as to grant all protection needed by our publishers, *provided, that the protection be not carried beyond that point.*

But there is one consideration on this subject, which is the most important of all, and which shows that the interests of the community, of authors, and of publishers, are identical; and that all would be injured by restrictions, of any sort, upon the importation of books. It is simply this, that the interests of all are promoted by a taste for reading. Everything that tends to promote such a taste, is subject for mutual congratulation, and everything which discourages it, injures all alike. It is too trite a truism to be gravely uttered, that the diffusion of knowledge is a benefit to the community; and yet, some would seem to doubt it; nay, as a nation, we have, by our legislation, implied a contrary opinion. We have thrown obstacles in the way of learning by preventing the free introduction of books. The cultivation of a taste for reading, while it benefits the whole community, is the very condition of existence for authors, and consequently for publishers.

A love for learning, and a taste for reading, are progressive and insatiable. They grow by what they feed on. The more books one reads, the more he wants to read. The greater the number of books circulated, the greater will be the demand for more. It is hardly possible that the market should be overstocked. A surfeit of good books has never yet occurred. Too many copies of even a good work, may be issued, but not too many different works, if each be better than its predecessor, on the same topic, and the topic one on which the community, or any considerable portion of it, are interested. Our community is, just now, in a forming state. A taste for reading must be developed. People must learn by experience how pleasant and useful a thing it is to read. To this end, they must be furnished with good books. They must, too, be furnished with them cheap, for so engrossed are we here with material pursuits, that we are not willing to pay much for pleasures, purely mental, which, as yet, we have hardly learned to prize.

The same principle applies to the introduction of works of art. Congress, with a laudable desire to encourage our artists, who have gone to Europe for the purpose of perfecting themselves in their profession, has exempted their works from the 20 per cent duty, which it imposes upon the works of foreign artists. So far, so good. But, by abolishing the duties on all works of art, it would, I believe, be confering a great additional favor upon those young men, who, sustained by no government patronage, and most of them destitute of private wealth, have gone abroad, fired with a noble enthusiasm for art, and relying upon their own exertions for success. What our artists most earnestly desire, for the community and in their own behalf, is the development of a love of art among the American people. This love of art can only be created, by spreading abroad among us the objects suited to awaken it. But, once created, it will, in time, become discriminating. Then, our artists will find the employment which they deserve. Do they fear, or do their friends fear for them, a competition with the artists of other nations? By no means. They cordially challenge such competition. Who, that has been in Florence, would not prefer a copy of Claude or Salvator, by our countryman, Brown, to one by any other artist whose works he can there obtain? And how many foreign artists are there, who can excel him in the masterly beauties of his original landscapes? Who, *in the world*, can make a better bust than Powers? How much has Crawford to fear from the creative genius of his competitors at Rome? Terry, and Huntington, and Loutze, are winning applause from men of all nations who examine their performances. The latter has taken several prizes from the Academy of Dusseldorf. I could speak in terms of equal commendation of others. America has produced a Stuart, A Copley, A West, an ALLSTON, and genius is no more a stranger to the soil of the western world than to that of classic Italy. All it wants is an appreciative taste in the community, and such a taste can only be created and cultivated by the free introduction of works of art.

Finally, if we look into the policy of other civilized nations, as to the introduction of books, we shall find much to shame us out of a virtually prohibitory system.

The Germanic Union, Denmark, Holland, Norway, Russia, and Spain, admit books duty free. Sweden and Portugal admit books, in foreign languages, duty free. Austria, Belgium, and France, lay upon them import duties. These duties are all specific. I have, however, made as near an estimate as possible, of the equivalent ad valorem duties, from data furnished by McGregor's reports to the British Parliament. The result, which is above rather than below the truth, is as follows:

Austria charges	2-1/2	per cent.
Belgium, do.	3	per cent.
France, do.	1	per cent. (on foreign books)
Great Britain,	12	per cent. (on foreign books)

Thus, we see, no one of these nations imposes a duty so high as the one proposed for us. Even Great Britain, where taxation is so oppressive, falls eight per cent short of our mark! But if these nations should exclude books, entirely, it would furnish us with no apology for doing the same thing. Each of them possesses the stores of her own and foreign literary treasures for centuries. Their vast libraries, their extensive and well organized book trade, their host of highly educated authors, render each of them intellectually rich, in and of herself. But we do not possess, in all our public libraries combined, books enough to meet the wants of a thorough scholar in any one of the great departments of human learning. And, as to our own productions, a single estimate will show our comparative poverty.

The whole number of different volumes published since the invention of the art of printing has been estimated at 3,000,000. Of these 1,000,000 are German, 800,000 French, 600,000 English, and only 25,000 American.

In view of these considerations, and the facts and statistics, upon which they are based, I would most respectfully suggest to the Library Committee, the propriety of immediate and energetic efforts to prevent any increase of the present duties, and, if possible, to secure—so far as it can be done consistently with the affording of a reasonable protection to American publishers, a repeal of all duties upon books.

C. C. Jewett

Brown University
March 31, 1846

A NATIONAL LIBRARY
FOR THE UNITED STATES

In his first annual report to the Board of Regents of the Smithsonian Institution, Charles Coffin Jewett launches his campaign for a "national library." He begins by carefully laying the foundation for a case that he obviously realized would need to be pressed over a number of years. Early in the report he compared American with European libraries, and concluded that while America had done much in the way of "diffusing" knowledge among the people, she had done little in providing the resources necessary for the "increase of knowledge"; that is, we had not built the great literary "treasure-houses" upon which all true scholarship must build. In this area we were far behind the Europeans.

Jewett presents tables and other evidence demonstrating that American scholars are at a serious disadvantage because of the lack of large libraries in which to work, and notes that this burden falls most heavily upon the poor scholar who is unable to study in Europe or build his own private collection. What was needed was a great national library, one that would serve the needs of all scholars, rich and poor alike, and that, he noted, was the "design of the Smithsonian Institution."

After establishing this ground, Jewett describes the ways in which he intends to accomplish his purpose, and in doing so makes a slight foray into a topic of considerable interest to him—subject bibliography. Finally, he returns to his central theme, and concludes with a flourish, arguing that the Smithsonian Library, if developed in the proper fashion, will contribute to easing party tensions and to lessening social strife, and would prove more valuable than "fleets and armies to true national dignity."

●   ●   ●

Source: *Third Annual Report of the Board of Regents of the Smithsonian Institution . . .* (Washington: Tippin and Streeper, Printers, 1849), pp. 34-47.

Report of the Assistant Secretary Relative to the Library, Presented December 13, 1848.

To the Secretary of the Smithsonian Institution:

Sir: At the last meeting of the Board of Regents the following duties were assigned to me for the year which is about to close, viz:

1. "The preparation of catalogues of books suitable for the commencement of the library, in accordance with the plan of organization adopted by the Board of Regents.

2. "The purchase of the more necessary works on bibliography.

3. "The collection and systematic arrangement for purposes of comparison of the printed catalogues of the principal libraries throughout the United States, together with information with regard to the expenditures, plans of increase, and other particulars relating to said libraries.

4. "The collection of works to which the institution may be entitled under the tenth section of the act establishing the Institution."

The first of these duties which demanded my attention after the adjournment of the Board of Regents, was the collection of the works to which the institution is entitled by the tenth section of the charter. After examining the subject carefully, I made a special report thereon to the Secretary and Library Committee, a copy of which is herewith submitted.

The next subject to which I devoted my attention was the gathering of information respecting public libraries in the United States. It is a singular, and to us a mortifying fact, that the most accurate account of American libraries was published in Germany, and has never been translated into English. In 1845,-'6 there appeared in the "Serapeum,*" a journal published at Leipzig, a series of articles upon bibliography and libraries in the United States. These articles, forming about ninety pages octavo, were written by Hermann E. Ludewig, formerly of Dresden, at present a lawyer in the city of New York. Having a strong predilection for bibliographical pursuits, he collected, during a journey which he performed through the United States, all the information within his reach respecting the libraries, public and private, the book trade, and the bibliography of the general and local history of the country. The results of his researches have been given to the public in the articles to which I have already referred, and in an 8vo. volume of 180 pages, published for private distribution, entitled, "The Literature of American Local History; a Bibliographical Essay; New York, 1846." The fullness and accuracy of the details which he has given are remarkable. I have made free use of them, and have found my labors much facilitated by so doing.

---

*Serapeum. Zeitschrift für Bibliothekwissenschaft, Handschriftenkunde, und aeltere Literatur. Heraus. von Dr. Robert Naumann, Leipzig, T. O. Weigel, 1840 ff. (See 1845, pp. 209-224, and 1846, pp. 113-172, 177-190, 190-192, 204-206.)

I have, besides, visited and examined many of the principal libraries. I have also prepared, for the purpose of eliciting further information, a circular letter to librarians, a copy of which accompanies this report. This letter was distributed together with the first volume of our "Contributions to Knowledge." I regret that the answers to the queries have not all been received, so that I am unable at present to offer a full report respecting them. The most important statistics have, however, been obtained. These are presented in an accompanying document. I beg leave here to offer some important deductions from the facts contained in this paper.

The aggregate number of volumes in the public libraries of the United States is about 1,294,000. These are distributed among 182 libraries. Forty-three of these libraries contain over 10,000 volumes each; nine over 20,000 each, and only two over 50,000. The library of Harvard University, the largest this side the Atlantic, contains, together with the libraries of the law school and divinity school, upwards of 70,000 volumes.

These statements enable us to institute an instructive comparison between our libraries and those of the principal nations of Europe. It should be premised, however, that it is a very difficult thing to procure exact statistics of libraries. With reference to France, Germany, Belgium, Russia, and Spain, we are in possession of comparatively accurate returns. With respect to Great Britain, Holland, Sweden, Denmark, and Norway, those which I give below are as accurate as I could procure, though certainly not very satisfactory. I am not acquainted with any book which gives a good account of the present condition of libraries in several of these countries except one,* to which I have not had access.

For greater convenience of reference and comparison, I present these statistics in a tabular form. (on page 80)

The first column of the table gives the name of the country.

The second, the year to which the statistics relate.

The third, the number of public libraries.

By public libraries are not meant those exclusively which are opened to the public without restriction, but rather those belonging to public institutions,

---

*I allude to the Archiv der Gesellschaft für aeltere deutsche Geschitskunde. Herausg. v. G. H. Periz. Bd. 8. Hannov, Hahn, 1843, 8°. Petzholdt in the Anzeiger für Literatur der Bibliothekwissenschaft for 1843, terms this an almost inexhaustible source of information on European Libraries.

Note – Since writing the above, I have received the volume alluded to. The information which it contains, though fully justifying the expression of Petzholdt, relates principally to the manuscript treasures of the libraries, and is not of a statistical character.

Since the report was prepared, I have seen in the Serapeum, a translation of parts of an article containing a statistical account of libraries in Europe and America, first published in the Journal of the Statistical Society of London, by Edward Edwards, esq., of the British Museum. The original article I have not as yet been able to procure. It appears to have been prepared with great care and a wide examination of authorities. It would doubtless have saved me much laborious research had I seen it before writing my report.

Comparative statistics of libraries in Germany, France, Great Britain, Russia, United States of America, Denmark, Belgium, Sweden, Spain, and Norway.

Name of the country.	Date of statistics.	No. of libraries.	Aggregate number of volumes.	No. of libraries with over ten thousand volumes.	Average size of libraries of over ten thousand volumes.	No. of volumes in the largest libraries.	Comparative number of books to the population. No. to every million inhabitants.
Germany, including Austria and Switzerland	1845	103	5,578,980	68	80,000	600,000	136,072
France	1844	241	4,771,000	121	35,000	800,000	145,000
Great Britain	1840	31	2,001,000	23	85,000	420,000	83,000
Russia	1843	120	1,321,115	16	69,000	464,000	28,000
United States of America	1847	182	1,294,000	43	17,000	70,000	64,000
Denmark	1840	13	660,000	5	123,000	400,000	330,000
Belgium	1841	31	614,722	16	35,000	100,000	153,000
Sweden	1841	16	358,000	7	43,000	150,000	120,000
Spain	1835	21	354,557	5	57,000	200,000	30,000
Norway	1842	14	157,783	2	74,000	126,000	150,000

and which are accessible under proper regulations to persons who wish to consult them for literary purposes.

The fourth column contains the aggregate number of volumes in the libraries.

The fifth gives the number of libraries containing over 10,000 volumes each.

The sixth, the average number of volumes in libraries containing over 10,000 volumes each.

The seventh, the number of volumes in the largest library of each country.

The eighth, the number of volumes to every million of inhabitants.

This table enables us to estimate at a glance, and with a good degree of accuracy the relative value of the public provisions made in Europe and America for general intellectual culture, as well as of those for the most extensive scientific and literary research.

It will be seen that in the *number of public libraries*, France is the only country in the world which excels us. It should be observed that the returns respecting France are official and minute, including libraries of not more than 500 volumes. Many of our public schools, however, possess libraries larger than these, but they are not enumerated in our lists. If they were, they would swell the number of American libraries far beyond that of any other country in the world.

In the aggregate number of volumes in the public libraries, Germany, France, Great Britain, and Russia, are before us. Were all the district school libraries and village collections in the United States included in the estimate, we should probably take the fourth rank.

In the average size of libraries containing over ten thousand volumes we are the *last of all*.

In the size of the largest library we also stand *last of all*.

In the number of volumes, compared with the population, we rank below all *but Russia and Spain*.

These results show that in public provisions for the general diffusion of knowledge by means of libraries, we stand in the very first rank among the nations; and when we consider the cheapness of our publications, and the vast number of them scattered over the land, with the extent of our periodical literature, we may justly and proudly challenge a comparison with any nation in the world for the means of general culture. This, certainly, is much for a country so new, whose chief energies have, as a matter of necessity, been directed to the felling of forests, the clearing of lands, and the support of physical life. It shows, as well remarked by a foreign writer, "that the men who, with steady and vigorous hand, have known how to rule themselves, and be completely free, have well discerned the foundations upon which alone the weal of a free State can safely repose."

But this deduction, so full of encouragement, so fraught with matter for gratulation and pride, must be followed by others of a different character.

The statistics given indicate, that while no country in the world has done so much for *diffusing* knowledge, none has done so little towards furnishing the means which public libraries can supply for its *increase*. It was doubtless the first duty of the infant republic to provide that all should know something, that the mass of the people should be elevated and enlightened. It has now become her duty to see to it, that no bounds are placed to the culture that each may obtain if he chooses. Now, in the hour of her strength, she ought to provide for her citizens the means of as high culture, of as profound research, of as noble advances in science, literature, and art, as are enjoyed by the citizens of any other nation in the world. She should take care that while the poor man's son may obtain that elementary education which will enable him to perform the duties of a good and intelligent citizen, he be not, by his poverty, debarred from the higher walks of science and literature; that there be no monopoly of learning by the rich—by those who are able to study at the institutions of Europe, or to surround themselves by the books which they need at home. Our condition in these respects has been deeply lamented by our scholars. At various times strong efforts have been made for its improvement. At length the munificent bequest of a foreigner, placed at the disposal of Congress, furnished the means of meeting this, among other demands of science and letters. In the act of Congress establishing the Smithsonian Institution, and in the acts of the Board of Regents for the organization of the same, a large public library forms a prominent feature.

It has been supposed by some, not acquainted with researches requiring many books, that very large libraries are superfluous. They calculate, perhaps, how many books a man can read in a long life, and ask what can be the use of more. Nay, even many men fond of reading feel like an English writer of some note, who describes his pain as amounting to "midsummer madness" when he entered a large library and reflected how small a number of all the books it contained he could read through.

"In my youthful days," says De Quincey, "I never entered a great library, say of 100,000 volumes, but my predominant feeling was one of pain and disturbance of mind, not much unlike that which drew tears from Xerxes, on reviewing his immense army, and reflecting that in 100 years no one soul would remain alive. To me, with respect to the books, the same effect would be brought about by my death. Here, said I, are 100,000 books, the worst of them capable of giving me some pleasure and instruction, and before I can have had time to extract the honey from one-twentieth of this hive, in all likelihood I shall be summoned away."

"Now I have been told by an eminent English author, that with respect to one single work, viz: the History of Thuanus, a calculation has been made by a Portuguese monk, which showed that barely to read over the works, and allowing no time for reflection, would require three years labor at the rate of, I think, three hours a day. Further, I had myself ascertained that to read a duodecimo volume in prose of four hundred pages, all skipping being barred, and the rapid reading which belongs to the vulgar interest of a novel, was a very sufficient work for one day. Consequently 365 per annum, that is with a very small allowance for the claims of life on one's own account and on that of one's friends, one thousand for every triennium, that is ten thousand in thirty years, will be as much as a man who lives for that only can hope to accomplish. From the age of twenty to eighty, the utmost he could hope to travel through would be twenty thousand volumes, a number not, perhaps, above five per cent. of what the mere current literature of Europe would accumulate in that period of years."

Now, supposing for a moment that there were no other use to be made of books but the reading of them through at so many pages the hour, one would think it might have occured to this writer that there are among the frequenters of a large library a great variety of men, with a wide diversity of interests, tastes and pursuits; that though each might not be able to read through more than two thousand books—one-tenth part of the supposed number—still fifty men, whose reading was in different directions, might call for a hundred thousand.

But apart from this consideration, and above it, is another of far more importance to the scholar. It is that this view of the use to be made of a large collection of books is founded upon an utter misapprehension of the relation of books and libraries to learning.

There are three uses to be made of books by those who understand their value.

The first is for *reading*. This, paradoxical as the assertion may sound, is the least important of their uses. By reading I mean cursory perusal, such as the writer above quoted describes. Reading as a pastime—reading for the acquiring of general information—reading as a means of refining and cultivating the tastes—is, indeed, indispensable to every well educated man. And the means of such reading in this country are largely supplied by our circulating libraries, athenaeums, book auctions, and cheap publications. But the scholar has need of books for other and higher purposes.

A second important use of books is for *study*. By study, I mean that vigorous mental application, which is necessary in order to fully comprehend, weigh, analyse, and appropriate the thoughts, facts, and arguments of an author. It is study which disciplines the mind; which trains the intellect for the rapid accumulation and appropriate use of knowledge. It is study which gives education, which developes the faculties. But it is evident that for study one needs even fewer books, if they be rightly chosen, than for reading.

The third use to be made of books is for *reference*.

Every man has occasion to refer to a dictionary or an encyclopedia. Yet who ever undertakes to read one through? Every one accustomed to composition sometimes has occasion to trace the history and meaning of a word. "There are cases," says Coleridge, "in which more knowledge or more value may be conveyed by the history of a word than by the history of a campaign." But to learn the history or usage of a single word we may be compelled to look into five, twenty, or fifty dictionaries in different languages.

Now the use of books by scholars is in general analogous to the use of a dictionary by any intelligent man. There are some sciences which seem to require less the aid of libraries than others. It may even be true that some important discoveries have been the result of mere accident. But such is not the general rule. The progress of science is not fortuitous. Nature does not often disclose her treasures upon a blundering invitation. She must be diligently sought. He who would make valuable discoveries, must, as a general thing, prepare himself by a thorough acquaintance with the present condition and tendencies of the science which he cultivates.

He must do more, much more. "Of every branch of the two great subdivisions of human learning," (viz: science and literature,) says an able writer, "its history is a constituent part, absolutely necessary to all who would be competent to form just opinions on its present state." He must know the past in order to appreciate the present, and in order to help shape the future. He must not only be able to place himself on the line of demarcation between the unknown and the known, but if he would penetrate the darkness of the former, he must have gained his direction by a careful tracing out of the analogies of the latter. Consequently he must give himself to long-continued, patient, laborious study of the history of science.

Moreover, it is not only necessary to study that science which one wishes to enlarge by his discoveries: he must be familiar with the subjects which are allied to it. But where can we find the limits of any science? All knowledge is bound together by an indissoluble, though sometimes an invisible bond. He who is versed in but one department of science, and is entirely ignorant of others, cannot be said to be thoroughly acquainted with any. In the words of the writer already quoted, "If books could be arranged in order of relevancy, with respect say to natural science, from the one which is most essential to it down to the one which is least essential to it, there would be no perceptible break anywhere, no point at which natural knowledge ends and other knowledge begins." What, then, must he who would devote himself to the enlargement of one department of knowledge, wait ere he commences till he has mastered all? By no means, such is not the inference. The legitimate conclusion from the argument is, that no thorough student in any one department of knowledge can safely say that he may not need 10,000, or even 50,000, books, and many of them of a character at first sight most remote from his path, not, indeed, for the purpose of reading or of studying them, but in order to settle, by momentary references, questions which may arise, the settling of which may be of the greatest importance to his progress.

If this be true with respect to those sciences where there is the least apparent want of books, much more is it so of those whose deductions are drawn from researches among the records of the past. The demands of the statesman, the jurist, the political economist, the historian, cannot be met without furnishing the materials for the widest investigation, nor always, indeed, those of the novelist or the poet. I have sometimes heard it said that the knowledge of the middle ages to be gained from one of the novels of Sir Walter Scott is far more valuable than that to be acquired from the perusal of a library of dusty tomes. But who that has ever lived was a more constant delver amidst the dusty lore of the past, in old libraries, among worm-eaten books, than the illustrious author of these volumes. He could not otherwise have produced them. Without the large libraries we could not have had the enchanting romance.

If it be asked, whether the libraries which we already possess are not sufficient to meet this demand, we reply, in the first place, that the large libraries of Europe, containing from 200,000 to 800,000 volumes, some of them selected with great care, have not been found large enough to meet the wants of her scholars, and we may not allow that our countrymen are less fond of learning, less thorough and profound in their investigations, when they have the means of pursuing them, than their transatlantic brethren.

It may, however, justly be supposed that the number of volumes is a very inadequate criterion of the value of a library; that a judicious selection may do much to compensate for numerical inferiority, and, consequently, that our libraries, although smaller, may be more useful to learning than the larger collections of Europe. This may be sufficiently answered by applying another and the most satisfactory method of testing the real value of our libraries; which is to take some works of acknowledged learning and importance, and inquire what books were necessary for their composition, and how many of them our public libraries can furnish? This process, it will be seen, is a tedious one. I have, however, pursued it in reference to a considerable number of books on a variety of subjects. Some of the results thus obtained may be stated in a few words, and they are fair specimens of all the others.

In Mr. Wheaton's History of International Law—a production which reflects great credit upon American talent and scholarship, and which procured for its lamented author the honor of election to the French Institute—139 works are referred to in the notes. A much larger number were, of course, consulted, many of which are mentioned in the body of the work. Thirty-nine among the most important and expensive of those which are formally cited, are not to be found in the largest law libraries in the United States. More than one-half of the remainder are common books, to be found in any well selected general library of 5,000 volumes. This work was written in Europe. It could not have been written in this country from the materials contained in our public libraries.

If we take a book of a different kind, demanding for its composition a thorough knowledge of the history of one of the physical sciences, and, consequently, requiring the assistance of authorities less accessible and of less general importance, the result will be all the more striking.

In the first volume of Hoefer's History of Chemistry, 251 works are referred to. Of these, about fifty are common books, to be found in almost any library of 5,000 volumes. Of the remaining 191, I cannot find 75 in all our public libraries.

•   •   •

From these facts it is manifest that there is no exaggeration in the language of one of the members of our Board of Regents, from South Carolina, who, in a report in the Senate in 1836, stated that "our whole body of literature, if collected in one place, would not afford the means of investigating one point of science or literature through all, or even a considerable portion of what has been written on it." Here, he adds, "where the foundations of government repose on the aggregate intelligence of the citizens, the assistance afforded by public institutions to the exertions of intellect is but one-tenth of that within the reach of the mind of civilized Europe."

The complaints of our scholars testify to our deficiency. Their wants have weighed heavily upon them. They have repressed genius. They may have condemned to oblivion names that would have rivalled the brightest in the history of science and letters. I might mention, it is true, Americans who have ranked among the most learned of the world. But they, like others less renowned, have had sorrowful experience of the deficiency of which we complain. They, however, in most instances, have, from their own private wealth, supplied the defects of public provisions. Had they been poor they would not generally have been the authors they were. They could not have had access to the necessary books, had they not possessed the wealth for buying them, or for crossing the Atlantic to consult them where they were already accumulated. The pages of our literary journals, the eloquent speeches elicited in Congress by the bills to establish the Smithsonian Institution, and the united voices of the friends of good letters throughout the land bear sad and unvarying testimony to our deficiencies.

Now, to supply these wants, or, in other words, to place American students on a footing with those of the most favored country of Europe, is the design of the Smithsonian Library.

●　　●　　●

The plan of collecting the library is as follows:

1. To purchase such books as may be needed by the various officers of the institution, and by persons preparing memoirs and reports for our publications, or engaged in researches under the direction of the Secretary.

2. To procure such works as may be required to render the institution a centre of bibliographical reference.

3. To procure a complete collection of the memoirs and transactions of learned societies throughout the world, and an entire series of the most important, scientific, and literary periodicals. The continuation of these may be obtained in exchange for our own publications.

4. The remaining funds of this department will be devoted to the purchase of books of general importance; at first, most especially those which are not to be found in other libraries of the country.

●　　●　　●

The importance of bibliographical studies is in this country but too little appreciated. In truth, the neglect of them is the most fruitful source of superficial, conceited, and rash authorship. On the continent of Europe, however, they are held in the highest esteem. This is doubtless one principal cause of the acknowledged superiority of the Germans in all matters requiring wide research.

Every student worthy of the name, when about to investigate a subject, wishes to know first what has been done by others in the same field.

Now, on almost every important branch of learning some diligent scholar has collected from the whole domain of literature the books pertaining thereto, arranged them for convenience of reference, analyzed their contents, and described their absolute and relative merit, with their external peculiarities and history. He has thus given a bibliography of that branch of knowledge. Such a work should manifestly be the first to be taken up, and among the last to be laid down by any one who would intelligently study that subject. A collection of such works, pertaining to all departments of knowledge, ought to be the first purchase for every general library.

Yet there is no respectable collection of them in any of our public libraries. The best is, I believe, that of Brown University, which contains but a few hundred volumes. Without question, therefore, by procuring the books necessary for carrying out the plan of making the library a centre of bibliographical reference, we shall furnish one class of books most immediately important to American scholars, as well as one most needed in making judicious selections for the future, and in aiding other libraries in the country in their choice of books.

●　　●　　●

In conclusion, I may add that the plans in operation for the library will, it is hoped, soon render it a valuable aid to American scholarship. Its sphere is quiet and unobtrusive, but none the less useful. Ere long it is destined, we hope, to rank among the largest, the best selected, and the most available literary treasure-houses of the world. Wherever such a collection is formed, be it in a large metropolis or a provincial town, thither students will resort. They will soon give tone and character to society around. Even in the great emporium of commerce, under the overshadowing power of trade, its influence would soon be recognized. Here, at the political centre of the nation, where assemble her statesmen and her orators, under a benignant sky, amid scenes consecrated in her history, a spot as accessible as any other from all parts of the country, is the most favorable location for a great library. Such a library will attract hither our scholars, now pursuing their investigations in Europe, or mourning at home over noble projects abandoned before the necessity of so long and expensive a pilgrimage. It will render Washington the centre of American learning. Its influences will descend noiselessly upon the community around, and spread in ever-widening circles over the land, softening the asperities of party contentions, calming the strifes of self interest, elevating the intellect above the passions and the senses, cherishing all the higher and nobler principles of our being, and thus contributing more than fleets and armies to true national dignity.

Respectfully submitted.

C. C. Jewett

ON THE ACQUISITION OF BOOKS
FOR THE NATIONAL LIBRARY

In his report for 1849, Jewett sounds the first of what was to be a continuing series of laments over the meager book budget of the Smithsonian. But he was generally undaunted, and he outlined three ways in which the Library might greatly enhance its collections: (1) through the generosity of private collectors, who, Jewett guessed, might own more and better books than all the public libraries in the country combined; (2) through exchanges with other institutions and countries; and (3) through the enforcement of the copyright deposit law. In the latter area, Jewett was the first in this country to fully realize the benefit of such a law, arguing that it promised to allow for the accumulation of a collection "complete, without a single omission." Unfortunately, he never was able to make the publishers fully comply with the law. Later Spofford, at the Library of Congress, was to make the system work just as Jewett had envisioned that it could.

Another important feature of the report is the brief notice of Jewett's idea for the preparation of a "general catalogue" of the libraries in the country. But above all he remains interested in pressing his case for a great national library to be located at the Smithsonian. The approach is familiar; first he notes that we may be "justly proud" of the many small libraries which dot the countryside, for, after all, "our institutions are founded upon the intelligence of *the many*; not upon the power, or wealth, or learning of the *few*." All that is now lacking is the large library to support in-depth scholarly research. Such a library could and should be built at the Smithsonian.

Once the case is again made, Jewett reveals some of his plans for developing the Library, and in doing so provides us with some real insights into the availability of books and the nature of the book trade in this country.

•　　•　　•

Source: *Fourth Annual Report of the Board of Regents of the Smithsonian Institution . . .* (Washington, 1850), pp. 32-43.

Second Report of the Assistant Secretary of the Smithsonian Institution, Relative to the Library—Presented Jan. 2, 1850

To the Secretary of the Smithsonian Institution:

Sir: In anticipation of the annual meeting of the Board of Regents, I beg leave to present to you the following report of operations during the year 1849, in the department committed to my care.

A rapid growth of the library during this period was not expected. We had not at our disposal funds for the extensive purchase of books. But although we have been compelled to postpone the fulfilment of our design in one of its most essential features, the delay has been improved in making arrangements which will greatly facilitate our future progress, and in advancing, to a degree which would not otherwise have been possible, the plans detailed in my last report, for rendering our library a centre of bibliographical reference.

•   •   •

The *purchases*, it will be seen, have been few, for the imperative reason already mentioned. They do not comprise all the books in either of the selections, which I had the honor to present last year; nor can we hope to buy them all with even another annual appropriation. It will be observed, too, that some books have been bought in other departments than those to which the selections mentioned were confined. For a large library, it is sometimes wise to depart from a plan of purchasing, which on general principles, may have been adopted as the best. The exigencies and opportunities of the book market may not only justify but demand such a departure. A collection of books which may have occupied in gathering it the best years of an active life, and the constant thoughts of a highly cultivated mind, may be offered to us at a low price. In buying it, we get not only the books, but the study and labor which were necessary for selecting and procuring them. Although, therefore, the collection be out of the line of our immediate plans, it should not, on that account alone, be refused. The temptations to swerve from an established system are, however, from this source, both numerous and strong; and good judgment is necessary to determine, in each case, the course to be pursued.

With reference to *donations*, those already received are believed to be no criterion by which to judge of our probable annual accessions from this source. It is not generally known that we are ready to receive such presents. No formal invitation for them has been issued. The history of all the libraries in this country is, however, singularly instructive upon this point. More than three-fourths of all the books in our public libraries are presents. Nearly the same thing may be said of some of the large libraries of Europe. Of 435,000 volumes in the British Museum, more than 250,000 were presented. Our situation in this respect is peculiarly promising. The seat of government of the United States must have an important and growing influence in literary affairs. There will always be among the officers of the government, the members of Congress, and the foreign diplomatic corps, men of high attainments in science and letters. Our institution will, we may hope, receive their warmest sympathy. During the sessions of Congress, there will be also a large concourse of visitors from our own and other lands, whose interest is strong in learning, and who will rejoice to find here the facilities for the gratification of their favorite tastes. There will thus, we may hope, grow up here, aside from political circles, a literary influence like that around many of the universities of Europe, and like that which has added so much lustre to the capital of Prussia. If we are true to our position, if we secure and retain the confidence of that part of the community most interested in our operations, we shall attract the donations and bequests of a wide and ever enlarging circle of friends of science and good letters. The meagreness of our public libraries has led men of wealth and of study to collect for themselves, in special departments, private libraries quite complete within the range to which they are limited. The aggregation of these libraries, as they now exist, would make perhaps a better library for research than could be formed by the union of all our public collections. It is not improbable that some of these will eventually be intrusted by their proprietors to the permanent guardianship of our institution. A scholar of adequate means nowhere, excepting in his own writings, presents to the world so good a representation of his tastes, pursuits, and attainments, as in the collections which he makes of the writings of others. His library shows the friends whom he chose, the companions in whom he delighted. It shows the range of his sympathies and the extent and minuteness of his investigations. It is the exponent of his intellectual life. It is associated with his severest struggles, his best aspirations, his noblest triumphs. He shrinks from the thought of its being scattered when he can no longer use it, and he seeks a safe depository where it may remain—the most enduring monument that can be erected to his learning and his munificence.

It is upon this honorable principle in the scholar's character that our hopes are founded. Such a depository as he seeks we wish to form here. Purchases of books, even were our whole income devoted to them alone, would never place us on an equal footing with the scholars of Europe. We have, however, other reliance. If we make a beginning; if we provide room, safe custody, and the proper facilities for rendering such a collection in the highest degree subservient to its legitimate purposes, private liberality will come vigorously to our aid.

Another source to which we may look for considerable accessions to our library, and one from which we have, as yet, little to report, is exchanges. The publications of the several State governments are numerous, and we can, without doubt, procure most of them by exchange and donation. The various learned societies to which we have presented copies of our first volume of Contributions, in thanking us for the gift, have assured us of their intention to send us their own memoirs and transactions in return. These will be of great value as the sources of current information in science and literature, and will go far towards remunerating us for the expense of our own publications. Even from libraries which put forth no regular publications, we have been promised valuable returns.

I herewith present a list of all the books, maps, charts, musical compositions, &c., deposited in our library by authors and proprietors, for the security of the copyright, in compliance with the requirement of the 10th section of the act of Congress establishing the institution. The whole number of volumes and other articles received, from the 10th of August, 1846, to the 1st of January, 1849, is 1,071. Of these, 521 (viz: 389 books, 94 pieces of music, and 38 other articles) were received from January 1 to December 31, 1849. I have no means of ascertaining the exact number of copyrights secured in the United States during this period. The system of record and deposit in the clerks' offices and State Department is such as to render it difficult, if not impossible, to ascertain with accuracy the statistics of this subject. The librarian of the copyright rooms of the State Department informs me that the number of books annually deposited there is about 400. This cannot be more, I think, than one half of the whole number for which copyrights are nominally secured each year in the United States.

For the first two years and a half from the date of our charter, but few publishers complied with the requirement of the act of Congress, so far as our institution was concerned. During the last year, however, the number has greatly increased; and now, we regularly receive the publications of most of the large publishing houses in the country. The mere cost of the books sent is not regarded by publishers; but the transmission of them is sometimes troublesome and expensive. If they could be forwarded without expense to the publishers, and if we could render the deposite more immediately advantageous, no doubt many more books would be sent to us.

To the public, the importance, immediate and prospective, of having a central depot, where all the products of the American press may be gathered, year by year, and preserved for reference, is very great. The interest with which those who in 1950 may consult this library would view a complete collection of all the works printed in America in 1850, can, only be fully and rightly estimated by the historian and bibliographer, who has sought in vain for the productions of the past. These publications should be kept apart from the rest of the library, in chronological order. They should be so marked that they may be readily and surely identified. They should be restricted to the library room, except when required in case of dispute respecting title; but they should be freely accessible to all who wish to consult them in the library. Thus, in coming years, the collection would form a documentary history of American letters, science and art. It is greatly to be desired, however, that the collection should be *complete, without a single omission.* We wish for every book, every pamphlet, every printed or engraved production, however apparently insignificant. Who can tell what may not be important in future centuries?

"It is in the fragments, now so rare and precious, of some alphabets, of some small grammars published for the use of schools about the middle of the 15th century, or in the letters distributed in Germany by the religious bodies commissioned to collect alms, that bibliographers now seek to discover the first processes employed by the inventors of xylography and typography. It is in a forgotten collection of indifferent plates, published at Venice by Fausto

Verantio, towards the end of the sixteenth century, that an engineer, who interests himself in the history of the mechanical arts, might find the first diagram of iron suspension bridges."–(*Libri*.)

But neither the collection of copyrights at the State Department, nor that in the library of Congress, nor our own, is complete, or approaching completeness. Thus, the historical and bibliographical importance of each is greatly diminished.

To publishers it is necessary, for the security of their property, that a certified copy of each work should somewhere be preserved. The depositing of the copy in the office of the district clerk for the State Department, has been by the Supreme Court of the United States declared to be essential to securing a valid copyright. Whether the same be true with reference to the copies required for our institution and the library of Congress, is a question of law which I am unable to answer. The interest of publishers, as well as of the public, seems to require additional and more explicit legislation on this subject.

●　　●　　●

GENERAL CATALOGUE OF AMERICAN LIBRARIES

An important part of the plan for rendering our library immediately useful to American scholars is the proposed general catalogue of the books contained in all our public libraries. I am not aware that such a thing has ever before been attempted on so large a scale. The Navy Department of the French government published, a few years ago, a general catalogue of the books belonging to the various libraries (eleven in number) connected with that department. This useful work is contained in five large octavo volumes.

The French Department of the Interior, a few years ago, ordered a general catalogue to be made of all the manuscripts in the public libraries of France, and considerable progress has been made in the work.

But nothing like a general catalogue of all the libraries of a country has ever, to my knowledge, been undertaken. It has indeed been found next to impossible to make a catalogue of the largest library of each country. Much less possible would it be to make a general catalogue of all the libraries. The project, however, has lately been discussed in England, as appears from the report and minutes of evidence of the Select Committee of the House of Commons on public libraries. The discussion may have been suggested by the plan proposed by our institution. Be this as it may, it resulted in a strong recommendation, on the part of the committee, of great attention to a *system of catalogues*, and a *central collection of catalogues*–objects which would seem too obviously important to require formal announcement, and yet which have been much disregarded. There are few countries, indeed, where a general catalogue would be at all practicable. It is not an easy task even here; but it is not impossible. To its accomplishment, I have, during the past year, devoted considerable time.

The plan of the work I gave in my last report. On this plan, fifty-five thousand titles have been prepared from printed catalogues, and four thousand have been transcribed.

The titles must, of course, partake of the imperfections of the catalogues from which they are derived. These are neither few nor small. I say this not for the purpose of finding fault with their compilers; such censure would often be misplaced and unjust. The fault for inaccurate catalogues is frequently attributable less to the librarians who make them, than to their employers, whose impatience will not brook the delay necessary for the preparation of a valuable catalogue, or whose false notions of economy lead them to select incompetent librarians because they will work cheaply or require competent ones to perform so many other duties, that they have not time to devote to the catalogue; or, finally, who cripple and trammel them by prescribing absurd and unsuitable systems. Were the original registries in all our library catalogues satisfactory, a better service could hardly be rendered to learning, in this country, than by completing and printing this general catalogue.

The work at present funishes us with a catalogue, in one alphabet, of several libraries in Washington, as well as in Cambridge. But we hope that it will be found practicable through the agency of the Smithsonian Institution, to secure a general uniformity among the various libraries in the preparation of catalogues, and to establish a system of *stereotyping them by separate titles*; which will enable each library to print annual editions of its catalogue, incorporating the titles of the last accessions to the collection; and which will enable us, by means of the same titles, to print a general catalogue of all the libraries. The adjustment of all the details of such a system must, of course, be the work of time, and it may be found impracticable for us to commence the enterprise until we have a printing office of our own.

•   •   •

The comparative statistics presented in my last report, though not so full as I desired, were sufficiently so to show the general condition of the country in comparison to that of other countries, with reference to the apparatus for extensive study, as well as to the means of a more superficial but a widely diffused general culture and enlightenment. That some books should be accessible to all who are disposed to read, is more important as a means of general education, than that vast collections should be offered to the learned few. Our own condition is that of the wide diffusion of facilities for general reading. We have a large number of libraries; they are widely scattered; they are freely open to the public; the conditions of their use are so easy that none are deprived of them who are disposed to use them aright. Of this we may be justly proud. It is strictly in accordance with the nature of our institutions that we should consult first for the education and mental improvement of the great body of the population. Our institutions are founded upon the intelligence of *the many*; not upon the power, or wealth, or learning of *the few*. The diffusion of knowledge is our safeguard. The common school, the village library, the cheap free press, are the supports, the guarantees, the champions of liberty. We shall never be found pleading for anything that interferes with these or abridges their usefulness. It is rather in their interest that we ask for the means of the highest literary acquisitions. The stream cannot rise higher than the fountain; if the source be not well supplied, the river fails. Teachers must have the facilities for learning; and as the standard of education is raised, higher attainments are demanded from teachers—attainments which cannot at present be made in this country by the aid of our public institutions. I use the word "teachers" in its widest acceptation, including all who attempt to instruct the public. It is in the appliances for thorough study, for original research, for independent investigation, that we are deficient. If a studious and reflecting American desires to review the history of the world, or some portion of it, from his American position, unless he be able to expend thousands of dollars in the purchase of books, he must abandon his design, for he cannot procure them from our public collections.

There has recently appeared from the American press, written by an American scholar, one of the most comprehensive, profound, and elegant works which has ever been published in the department of literary history. We receive it with patriotic pride. But this work could be written, in this country, only by one who was able to procure for himself the necessary literary apparatus. The library of the author [George Ticknor] contains some 13,000 volumes, and in the department of Spanish literature is one of the richest in the world. Our object is to provide that *every man* in America, though he be poor, whose mind kindles with a great theme, may be able to pursue it and enrich our national literature with the results of original investigations. It is sometimes said, in reply, that if any one desires books not already to be found, he may order them from Europe, and receive them in six weeks or two months. But the scholar may be, and generally is, poor. If not, he cannot, from the outset, foresee the extent of the field over which he must range, the side-paths which he must trace out in order to settle the true route; he will thus be subjected to great delay in ascertaining and collecting his materials. But the ordering of books is a very different matter from what is generally supposed. If the book be a new one, still in the market, it may be received within a few weeks; but if, as is the case with two-thirds, or perhaps nine-tenths of the books which may be needed, it be an old work, and only to be found at long intervals and by diligent search, the case is very different. His order will be answered only by the phrase, "out of print." He may order again, and receive for reply, "cannot be obtained." This will be his experience till he devotes years to gathering his materials, or till, discouraged by his ill success, he abandons his design and sinks down to be a mere copyist and compiler; to take his opinions at second-hand, from perhaps superficial and prejudiced writers—the only ones to whom he can gain access. We are thus, as a nation, condemned to literary dependence, if not imbecility.

The government, and the educated men of every State in Europe, have felt the importance of having at least one library in each country, where the materials for thorough scholarship should be garnered, and opened to the studious; yet no nation in Europe is in a situation so much demanding such a collection as ourselves. If Roscoe could not obtain, as has been stated, in England, the books which he wanted for writing the history of Leo X, it was comparatively easy for him to cross the channel and consult larger collections on the continent; but for our authors a voyage of several thousand miles, and the expense of a residence abroad, are almost insurmountable barriers to literary exertion.

To lay the foundations of a large library is not a short nor an easy task. Few persons, even among learned man, estimate its difficulties aright. Much time and labor must be expended with but small immediate results. Patience and toil must be exercised by those intrusted with the task, and tolerated, if not appreciated, by the public. The history of similar institutions must be studied in order to avoid their mistakes, and profit by their successful experience. Lists of books must be made by a diligent study of the literature of every department of knowledge, and a wide consultation with men profoundly acquainted with each. Plans must be formed, not merely for the moment, and to meet temporary exigencies, but such as are capable of indefinite extension; such as will not require to be remodelled even when the library is expanded to its greatest magnitude.

How much expense, delay, mortification, and complaint might have been spared, had the directors of the large libraries of Europe, from the outset, foreseen and provided for the great enlargement of these establishments.

The large public library is, in truth, a modern, a *new* institution. It is only within the last half century that the uses of such libraries have been fully understood and appreciated, and the method of forming and conducting them studied upon true principles, and with satisfactory results. The public libraries of the ancients, and those of later times down nearly to the present century, were, as aids to learning, or means of popular progress in knowledge, not to be compared with those of our own day.

Books, as Voltaire has well said, rule the whole civilized world. But so rapid has been of late years the multiplication of them, that few scholars indeed can procure, by their own private resources, all that they need for their investigations. Yet, with the multiplication of books has increased the number which it is necessary for every one to consult who would not be behind the age in his learning. Hence public libraries have become an indispensable requisite to the attainment of liberal scholarship. The books in a public library cannot, however, be so well known to any particular student as those of his own shelves, nor can they be equally accessible to him; for he is not the only one who has a right to them, nor is it his convenience alone that is to be consulted. Hence arises the importance of so arranging, cataloguing, and keeping the library, as to facilitate the researches of each; without prejudice to the claim of any, or to the transmission of the privilege unimpaired to others. That the meeting of all these demands is no light matter, may be inferred from the fact that it has been made the serious study of some of the ablest minds in Europe; that its principles have been in Germany so thoroughly discussed and reduced to system, as, within the last twenty years, to have claimed admission into the family of the sciences.

It was in view of considerations like these, that the plans of the Smithsonian Library were made to embrace the early accumulation of works for bibliographical reference on all branches of learning; the collection of information respecting existing libraries of this and of other countries; the opening of a correspondence with these libraries for the interchange of opinions, and for mutual aid and encouragement, as well as the novel and important project of forming a central catalogue of all the different works to be found in the public, and, as far as practicable, the private libraries of the country.

Nothing of course can fully compensate for the want of books; but while we are gathering them slowly, and waiting for the means of more rapid accumulation, these plans will, it is believed, promote the immediate usefulness of our institution, and prepare the way for the ampler realization of our hopes with respect to it in the future.

Respectfully submitted.

C. C. Jewett

January 1, 1850

A NATIONAL UNION CATALOG
OF AMERICAN LIBRARIES

In his report for 1850, Jewett takes some pains to justify the existence of a great national library in Washington, answering the doubts of those who questioned the "appropriateness of this location for such an Institution." However, the majority of his report is devoted to a full account of his stereotype catalog plan.

After outlining the reasons for creating a national union catalog, and underlining the significance of catalogs to libraries, he describes his plan at length. Jewett was particularly aware of the problems associated with catalog production. He knew that printed book catalogs—to his mind the most appropriate kind—were expensive, quickly outdated, and awkward to use if frequently supplemented. His stereotype catalog plan was designed to provide both a national union list, and a means whereby other libraries could produce book catalogs of their own collections at a reasonable cost.

Jewett evidently was thinking of this idea as early as 1847. By 1850 he had his plan ready, and it was presented to the "Commissioners appointed to examine the plan for forming a General Stereotype Catalogue of the Public Libraries in the United States." This commission was made up of Edward Everett, Joseph Green Cogswell, Charles Folsom, Samuel Haven, Edward E. Hale, and George Livermore—all well-known librarians or bookmen—and they readily endorsed the plan. Jewett was then given the authority to experiment on a larger scale with his idea.

This report was written before much progress had been made, but it is important since it reveals Jewett's perceptive grasp of the bibliographic needs of the nation's libraries, and since it testifies to the primacy of his ideas on such matters as a national union catalog, an annual catalog of new books published in the country, and the equivalent of modern-day library book selection tools.

The portions of the report that deal at length with the mechanics of the stereotype scheme have been omitted here. They are covered very nicely in his address to the Librarians' Conference of 1853 and in the preface to his *On the Construction of Catalogues*, selections 9 and 10 in this volume.

●　　●　　●

Source: *Fifth Annual Report of the Board of Regents of the Smithsonian Institution . . .* (Washington, 1851), pp. 28-41.

Report of the Assistant Secretary in Charge of the Library of the Smithsonian Institution for the Year 1850

• • •

The experience of the last year would seem to decide the question of the appropriateness of this location for such an Institution. An establishment like this must have a fixed position somewhere. Yet its benefits are for all; not for one city nor one section of country, nor one nation even, but for "MANKIND". It is not to be denied, that a large city, like New York, or Philadelphia, or Boston, offers many advantages for the operations of such an Institution, not possessed by this city. It is, nevertheless, almost beyond question, that the comparison of advantages is in favor of this very place. There is no spot which presents so many attractions for the class of men most immediately interested in its concerns; no city, which they more gladly visit. The high officers of state, and the foreign diplomatic corps reside here. Here are held the sessions of Congress. Here are the executive departments of the government, the Patent Office, the Office of the Coast Survey and the Observatory. Every man, throughout the whole extent of the land, feels that here he has a friend,—a representative,— through whom he may communicate with such an establishment, when he cannot visit it in person. The facilities for the kind of intercourse, which we need with other countries, are, by the help of the State Department and of Foreign Ministers, greater than at any other point. More than all, the establishment here possesses a character of nationality, which would not elsewhere attach to its movement, in the eyes of our own people and of foreigners. This it was, undoubtedly, which led its founder to direct that the Institution should be established in Washington. Besides all this, it is enabled to multiply its influence and usefulness, by acting in concert with the departments of the National Government.

The inhabitants of a city where such an institution is established must, of necessity, share more largely in its benefits than others more remote. It is gratifying to know that this advantage could fall nowhere more appropriately, more benignly, or less invidiously, than upon this city. Selected and planned as for the seat of government of a mighty empire—a spot where nature laid her hand most gracefully—Washington has not hitherto been able, like her sister cities, to gather from commerce, wealth for endowments of learning. From the nature of our political institutions, she has been deprived, too, of that fostering munificence, which in Europe has reared splendid capitals from the sandy plain, or sunken morass, and supplied them not only with all that can meet the convenience and gratify the taste of their inhabitants, but also with Universities, Scientific Societies, and Libraries, for the advancement of civilization, refinement, and human happiness.

The central position and national character of the institution, have suggested many ways of rendering the Smithsonian Library useful to the literary public other than in the collection of books. These are not of course supposed to dispense with the importance of collections, nor do those which we have thus far adopted materially diminish our means of accumulation. They are additional objects of attention and they neither exclude nor interfere with the principal object. During the first years of the Library, while the money is wanting for extensive purchases, these plans receive a larger *relative* share of attention than may permanently be given to them; though it is hoped that they will actually continue to increase in extent as in importance.

One of these means of usefulness, was the gathering of statistical and historical notices of public libraries in the United States. This occupied a portion of my time during the year 1849. The results of my labors were presented in the appendix to my last report, which has not yet been printed. In establishing a central bibliographical bureau, it was of primary importance to survey the field in order to learn the number, condition, and prospects of existing libraries, and to establish with them, relations indispensable to success in any general system of operations.

GENERAL CATALOGUE

The formation of the General Catalogue of American Libraries has been another prominent object of my attention. As most of our public libraries possess printed catalogues, it is possible to form one central catalogue, by combining the titles of these, in one alphabetical arrangement. The value of such a work would be, in a measure, limited to this spot. The only way in which it could be extended further, would be by correspondence. Even thus limited, the scheme is very promising. It is manifest, however, that its benefits would be vastly increased, if copies of the catalogue could be multiplied. The catalogues of the different libraries were, however, constructed on plans so various, and in most cases, so faulty, that it was unadvisable to print any catalogue formed from them.

In order to realize from a general catalogue all of the vast advantages which it seems to promise, it is necessary that the catalogues of all the libraries of which it is composed, should be prepared with uniformity and accuracy; and in order to secure the co-operation necessary to the construction of catalogues in this manner, some plan must be devised, which would not increase, but if possible, diminish the present cost to each library of making and printing its catalogue.

•   •   •

It can hardly be necessary for me to dwell at length upon the benefits to be expected from a general printed catalogue of all books in the public Libraries of America. By means of it, every student in America would have the means of knowing the full extent of his resources for investigation. The places where the book could be found, would be indicated in the catalogue. A correspondence would be kept up between this Institution and every other library in the country. A system of exchange and of general loans might, with certain stringent conditions, be established, so that all the literary treasures of the country would be measurably accessible to every scholar. When the loan of a book would be impossible, extracts could be copied, quotations verified, and researches made, through the intervention of this Institution, which would in many cases be nearly as valuable to the student as the personal examination of the book.

In connection with this topic I would add: By law, a copy of every book for which a copyright shall be secured in this country is required to be delivered to the Smithsonian Institution, and to be preserved therein. It is hoped that additional legislation on this subject, will, while it lightens the burdens of publishers, secure the observance of this law, with respect to the Smithsonian Institution, *in all cases*. If then, the books thus obtained be all preserved, they will constitute the complete monumental history of American literature, during the existence of the law. It is useless to enlarge upon the value of such a collection.

If, now, a list of these publications, as they come into the library, should month by month be published in the proposed *BULLETIN*, and the titles immediately stereotyped, the expense would be trifling of publishing every year a catalogue of the books copyrighted in America during the year, and to print every five years, a general catalogue of American publications up to that limit. Thus, the monthly bulletins, the annual lists, and the quinquennial catalogues would furnish full and satisfactory records of American publications.

Again, this general catalogue would enable purchasers of books for public libraries, to consult, judiciously, for the wants of the country. So poor are we in the books which scholars need; so long, at best, must we remain in a condition of provincial dependence in literary matters; that a responsibility to the whole country rests upon the man who selects the books for any public library.

Another important benefit of this system is that it allows us to vary the form of the catalogue, at will, from the alphabetical to the classed, and to modify the classification as we please. The titles, separately stereotyped, may change their order at command. If, for example, it were required to print a separate list of all books in the country on the subject of *meteorology*, it would be necessary merely to check off in the general catalogue the titles to be used, and to hand it to the printer to do the rest of the work.

Another great benefit of this project would be to secure *uniformity* in catalogues. A good degree of uniformity would be absolutely indispensable to the success of the plan. Entire uniformity is not indeed to be expected. Perfection is not an attribute of the works of man. But a much higher degree of uniformity would result from this plan, than could otherwise be hoped for. The rules for cataloguing must be stringent, and should meet as far as possible all difficulties of detail. Nothing, so far as can be avoided, should be left to the individual taste or judgment of the cataloguer. He should be a man of sufficient learning, accuracy and fidelity, to apply the rules. In cases of doubt, reference should be made to the central establishment to which the whole work should be submitted, page by page, for examination and revision. Thus we should have all our catalogues formed substantially on one plan. Now, even if the plan adopted were that of the worst of our catalogues, if all were on the same plan, this uniformity would render catalogues, thus made, far more useful than the present chaos of irregularities. But we hope that the best possible system may be adopted.

Another general consideration is that this project looks towards the accomplishment of that cherished dream of scholars, *a universal catalogue.* If the system should be successful in this country, it may eventually be so in every country of Europe. When all shall have adopted and carried out the plan, each for itself, the aggregate of the general catalogues thus formed—few in number—will embrace the whole body of literature extant, and from them, it will be no impossible task to digest and publish a universal bibliography. How much this would promote the progress of knowledge by showing, more distinctly, what has been attempted and accomplished, and what yet remains to be achieved, and by thus directing the outlay of intellect aright; how much, by rebuking the rashness which rushes into authorship, ignorant of what others have written, and adding to the mass of books without adding to the sum of knowledge; how much by giving confidence to the true and heroic student, who fears no labor so that it bring him to the commanding height at which he aims—the summit of learning in the branch to which he devotes himself; how much such a work would, in these and other ways, promote the great object we have in view, is well deserving the attention of every thoughtful mind. Upon it I may not at present longer dwell.

In America alone can this system be put into immediate operation. In every large country in Europe the arrears in cataloguing, or the mass of titles accumulated in the libraries, would render the first expenses of the enterprise quite startling. But here all things conspire in our favor—our libraries are all small, and mostly repetitions one of another. But they are prosperous and will rapidly increase. Their supporters are all desirous of having printed catalogues. A central administration is necessary. This can be accepted by the Smithsonian Institution, whose position is peculiarly favorable, and whose funds are consecrated to such purposes. The enterprise requires no great outlay of money, no gigantic effort. It may go noiselessly, but rapidly into operation. There is nothing to prevent its immediate usefulness.

The commissioners appointed to examine and report upon the project, considered not only its general features, but also its minute details. To them were submitted the rules proposed for cataloguing, which were separately discussed, and after having been variously amended and modified, were recommended for adoption. It is not supposed that this code provides for every case that will occur. The peculiarities of books are, like the idiosyncracies of authors, innumerable. They baffle the best efforts at classification, except under general heads. The most elaborately formed laws for recording their titles would be inadequate to provide for entire uniformity or consistency. Doubts and difficulties would inevitably arise as to the application of the laws. These must, to prevent varying decisions, be submitted to one person. Hence it is important that the first part of the work, which will furnish examples for the rest, should be done under the immediate eye of the superintendent.

Easy as the operation may seem, to those who have never attempted it, there is no species of literary labor so difficult, or that requires knowledge so extensive and various, as the cataloguing of a large library. It demands peculiar qualifications of patience and accuracy, and a special education—a professional training. Even those most expert must work slowly, if they would avoid mistakes. It is therefore a great consideration that, on this plan, each title, once prepared, is prepared for all the libraries in which the book occurs; whereas, on any other, time and thought and labor are repeated for every copy of the book.

From the favor with which the plan has been met, it can hardly be doubted that it will receive the hearty and vigorous co-operation of all the libraries in the country. Several are ready to begin upon their catalogues at once. For the reasons already stated, however, it is desirable to begin here. At first the work cannot proceed rapidly. After the accumulation of a considerable number of titles, progress will be much accelerated.

Great as this enterprise is, it will not require the outlay of much money on the part of the Smithsonian Institution to put it in operation, which being once done, it will take care of itself. It will not be a constant drain upon our funds; but on the contrary, it will ere long far more than repay in the facilities for making our own catalogues, all that may at first be expended upon it.

Respectfully submitted,

Charles C. Jewett

December 31, 1850

THE CONTINUING DREAM
OF A NATIONAL LIBRARY

In this last selection from Jewett's annual reports to the Board of Regents of the Smithsonian, we find him ranging widely across a number of significant themes—all of them connected by the national library idea. While disappointed about the lack of funds for the purchase of books and by the failure of the copyright deposit system to function properly, he still appeared optimistic about the future of the Smithsonian Library.

His optimism in print might have exceeded somewhat his real feelings about the "great library" plan, for Jewett was now well aware of the intent of Secretary Henry to limit the development of the Smithsonian Library. However, he remained as determined as ever, and presented one of his most eloquent statements in support of the national library idea, concluding that "we may hope that money will not be wanting to establish the independence of American learning, to render it no longer provincial, no longer relying for its support upon the libraries of Europe."

•   •   •

Report of the Assistant Secretary, In Charge of the Library Presented January, 1853.

•   •   •

The number of articles received under the copyright law is somewhat larger for the last, than for the preceding year. It has increased from year to year since the organization of the Institution, although no special efforts have been made to induce publishers to comply with the law. Every book which has been

Source: *Seventh Annual Report of the Board of Regents of the Smithsonian Institution* . . . (Washington: Robert Armstrong, Printer, 1853), pp. 32-44.

received has been immediately and carefully recorded, and a certificate of deposit sent (generally by return of mail) to the depositor. The same care has been exercised for the most insignificant as for the most important; and has been dictated by a sense of justice to the publishers, inasmuch as the deposit was supposed to be essential to the perfection of their title. Had the articles thus sent been regarded merely as donations to the library, many of them might have been differently treated. Loose sheets of music, school-books, and many "cheap publications," might merely have been placed together in some spot where they would long have remained undisturbed. For themselves, and as parts of an imperfect collection, they were hardly worth recording. It should be particularly observed that any article, however apparently worthless, acquires value and importance as an integral part of a complete collection. A collection of all the productions of the American press would, if perfect and entire, teach lessons which could not be gleaned from its parts.

It would show the *extent* of the literary labors of the time.

It would show the proportionate attention to the various departments of learning.

It would show, from year to year, the increase or decrease of interest in particular pursuits.

It would show the comparative literary fertility and wealth of different portions of the country.

It would show the progressive improvements in the subsidiary arts of paper-making, binding, engraving, and so forth.

All these points possess interest to different classes of inquirers. The wants of all literary investigators should be respected, and, as far as possible, supplied. The historian is not less to be provided for than the philosopher, the artist than the statesman. If we had the means, therefore, of forming a complete collection of copyright works, we would reject nothing, not even that which might to ourselves appear utterly trivial and unworthy of preservation; for the article which one would reject, might, in coming times, for some reason which could not possibly have been foreseen, possess more interest than any other in the collection.

It is impossible for any man to judge competently of the wants of future generations. It is unsafe to intrust to any one the power of rejecting works as worthless. Many enlightened contemporaries of Milton and Newton would have rejected, as worthless, the Paradise Lost and the Principia. Sir Thomas Bodley, the founder of the great library which bears his name—a contemporary of Shakspeare—insisted, contrary to the advice of his librarian, Dr. James, in excluding plays and almanacs, and most pamphlets, which he was accustomed to call "riff-raff" and "baggage-books." The Bodleian Library is now paying very high prices for those books which then might have been procured almost without cost.

It is stated that one of the libraries in England, to which books were sent by copyright, and which was allowed to select such as were worthy to be retained, rejected, in a single year, The Antiquary; Mrs. Opie's novels; one of Wordsworth's odes, and his letter to a friend of Burns; Cobbett's publications;

Jameson on Minerals, (second edition,) and the Edinburgh Medical and Surgical Journal; The Siege of Corinth, and Shelley's Alastor; Lord Brougham's Speech on Agricultural Distress, and McCulloch's Essay on the National Debt; Comparative Tables of Commercial Weights; Beethoven's Musical Compositions, and many other similar works. (See "Copy of a Representation from the Trustees of the British Museum to the Treasury" March 27, 1846, page 35.)

There ought, therefore, to be in every country one complete collection of everything published—one library, where everything printed should be garnered up, and treated as of some importance; for, although in the multitude of libraries everything may be preserved somewhere, yet, from being scattered about, and from there being no one place where the student would be sure of finding all that he might seek, many books would be practically lost.

The investigator of the last half century of American history is now obliged to travel the country through to collect books and papers for his work. Suppose that everything published in the country for the last hundred years had been preserved in one library, had that library been in town or country, in the remote east or farthest south, it would have been the great place of resort for students of American history.

How many would already have gained among its alcoves the means of presenting to the world, in new and fresh pictures, the eventful history of our country. How many disputed and doubtful points would have been settled. How many errors would have been avoided. How much injustice to private character would have been silenced. How many bright examples of patriotism and devotion, now lost, would have been held up to the emulation of youth and the admiration of all.

Although these remarks go to show the importance of a complete collection somewhere, they do not show that the same rule of accepting or rejecting should be followed where it is known that the collection can never be made complete.

Every partial collection is supposed to be a selection made for some specific purpose; and although many works, apparently very remote in their character from those chosen, may be desirable, yet, when means of procuring and preserving are limited, it may be best, it may be necessary, to confine the selection to such as are most intimately connected with the main purpose of the library.

It might further be a question whether, admitting the importance of a complete collection of copyright books, it should be made here.

I endeavored to show, in my last report, that it would not be practicable to collect these books in any other way than by a condition of the copyright law, enforcing the deposit somewhere.

It seems appropriate, if not necessary, that the place of deposit designated by government should be at Washington. Experience has shown that the selection of the Department of State for this purpose is inconvenient. The President of the United States, in his last message to Congress, has expressed the opinion that it would be a benefit to the public service to transfer the execution of the copyright law from the State Department. The other places of deposit would be the library of Congress, and the Smithsonian Institution. Whether the deposit be made here, or in the library of Congress, it certainly is the duty of the government to defray all expenses connected with it. It pertains to the government, is a necessary condition of the protection which the government promises to authors, and is precisely analogous to the case of the deposit of models in the Patent Office. This Institution cannot afford, at its own cost, to receive and take care of everything that is deposited. At the same time it is bound, by its position, to urge the necessity of the deposit, to show how it should be regulated, and to do all that it can, without prejudice to its other interests, to secure to authors and to publishers, as well as to students and literary men, the full advantages which the law contemplates. I accordingly proposed last year a plan which seemed to me to meet all the necessities of the case.

The general features of this plan were:

1. To dispense with the registration of title, rendering the publication of the claim of copyright the only preliminary to the vesting of the right, previous to the depositing of a copy.

2. To reduce the number of copies required for deposit from three to one.

3. To require the deposit of one copy, at the risk and expense of the proprietor of the copyright, within a reasonable time after publication.

4. To require a small fee from the proprietor, sufficient to defray the expense of furnishing certificates, keeping records, and preserving the books. This fee might be made considerably less than that now required of publishers, and still meet all these purposes.

Thus the trouble and expense to publishers would be greatly diminished, without devolving any burden either upon government, or the Institution receiving the deposits.

The deposit in the library of this Institution might be made of great incidental benefit to publishers and authors.

It has been proposed to issue a monthly bulletin, to contain the list of all books deposited during the preceding month. This work might, under the operation of such a law as proposed, be commenced immediately. It would be widely circulated in this country, and among reading and studious men in all parts of the world. Publishers would generally be willing to pay a large price for such a medium of advertising. But, in the case supposed, the advertisement would be incidental to the deposit, and would cost them nothing. By our system of stereotyping the titles separately, they would not only fill their place in the bulletin, but would serve for the catalogue of our own library, and of every other possessing the books and receiving from us its printed catalogue.

Various attempts have been made to make complete lists of American publications; but although some have been quite full, none have ever been complete. The best is that of Mr. Norton, in the Literary Gazette.

It would be matter of surprise to many, and of patriotic pride to all, to know the interest with which this list is received in Europe. But a few years have elapsed since an English review arrogantly asked, "In the four quarters of the world, who reads an American book?" It would not now be more arrogant in us to demand, What citizen of the great republic of letters does not read American books?

On the presentation of my last report, I hoped that it would be printed and distributed early in the year among publishers and authors, that we might be able ere this time to ascertain fully their views on the subject. They are more immediately interested in the matter, and nothing should be done which would be unsatisfactory to them.

There is in this connexion another idea, which long ago occurred to me, but which I have not ventured to suggest openly, lest it should seem extravagant, and because I could see no immediate means for accomplishing the object; I mean an international copyright exchange.

If, for example, a duplicate collection of all works for which copyrights are secured in this country could be made, it might be offered to England in exchange for a like collection of its own publications; and this exchange, if prosperous between two countries, might be extended to all the principal nations of the book-making world. I do not propose any plan for effecting this end, nor do I know that it could ever be realized; but in view of what has been done by this Institution during the last year in the way of literary exchanges, such an idea is not altogether chimerical. The advantages which would result from such an interchange would be immense. The literary and scientific labors of each country would be known in their full extent, and almost simultaneously in all other countries. Would not science advance more rapidly? Would not better justice be done to American genius?

Nothing, it seems to me, could more effectually conduce to the rapid progress of science and humanity, than a system which should make the literary and scientific labors in each country known immediately in all others.

The books gathered would, it is true, be in but one library; but books in a large public library, though chained to the shelves, are not to be shut out from the world. They contain ideas, which entering the minds of those who have access to them, there fructify, and the fruit is scattered far and wide. Books, it is true, are silent and motionless: they seem to produce no results. But within them is the spring of all progress, the spirit which stimulates and sustains all the activity that the world of letters, of science, of politics, and of religion, manifests.

The number of books purchased during the last year is very small. The money was especially desired for the successful completion of enterprises undertaken by the department of active operations. Besides this, the rooms temporarily occupied as a place of deposit for books were, even at the beginning of the year, filled nearly to the capacity of the shelves erected, and it was thought best not to incur further expense for arrangements which could not be of permanent utility.

The selection of books for purchase has been uniformly of such as were immediately needed, not of such as might be more remotely useful. It would have been preposterous to attempt with our means the immediate formation of a universal library; though we have not ceased to cherish the hope and belief that a great library of reference and research will ultimately be gathered here.

Our expectations for the library are not limited by our immediate means of purchasing books. The history of other libraries in this country shows that any permanent and well located institution of the kind may reasonably expect accessions by donation and bequest, in proportion to the importance of its position. The more conspicuous, central, and permanent the establishment, the more likely it is to attract the liberal notice of those who have valuable collections to bestow.

The location of the Smithsonian Institution at Washington, its permanent endowment, its independence of partisan and sectarian influences, the high position in the scientific world which it has already achieved by its active operations, the results of the system of exchanges of which we are now enjoying but the first fruits, together with the various means which have been adopted or suggested for aiding other libraries and advancing bibliographical objects, conspire to give prominence to the library of this Institution; and they will, before many years, render it, if not the largest and most important in the country, at least a very valuable auxiliary to our national literary progress. We expect, however, that it will increase mostly by exchanges and gifts. We may justly hope that many valuable private collections of books in particular departments of learning will be placed here, to remain as the best monument that can be reared to commemorate the learning and taste as well as the liberality of their collectors.

It is not the love of acquisition or pride of possession which leads us to desire such gifts. It certainly is not the wish to withdraw them from other institutions. It is the belief that a large library of reference is likely to be formed here, and to be more generally useful here than if placed in any other city. There is no city in the Union more attractive to men of science and letters than Washington. This is principally owing to the fact that so many of the most intellectual men of the nation are gathered here, occupying its high places of trust and honor, and that here are discussed, by statesmen and orators, questions of deepest interest to liberty and civilization. The attractiveness of Washington is enhanced by its genial climate, which will undoubtedly render it more and more a favorite resort. This Institution, from its location, its connexion with the government, and its own organization and operations, possesses opportunities for collecting certain classes of books, which are of great importance in a library of reference, superior to those of any other library except that of Congress. I refer to memoirs and transactions of learned societies, publications of educational establishments, documents of the general and State governments, and of foreign governments, besides many pamphlets and books, principally of local character, published in all parts of the land.

We do not suppose that here, or anywhere, for many years to come, will be formed that complete treasury of the materials for literary pursuits which is the beau-ideal of the bibliographer; but we may, nevertheless, do all that we can (without prejudice to other interest) in the direction of this desirable end.

It is proper to remark, in this connexion, that the chief expense of a library is not in the permanent custody of it when once rightly ordered. It is in the care of accessions, and the establishment of them as parts of the collection. Every book which comes into a library must be subjected to the following processes: It must be collated, to see that it is perfect; stamped, so that it can be identified; recorded in the book which constitutes the inventory of property; located upon the shelf, and have its location marked upon it; entered in the local catalogue, which shows the books upon each shelf, and enables the librarian to discover the title of any one that may have occupied a spot now vacant. It must also be catalogued and indexed: perhaps its receipt must be acknowledged to the donor; and it may require to be marked for binding. It is this work upon all accessions, which is repeated for every pamphlet and every article—the work of organizing a library, together with that of selecting books and directing purchases—which constitutes the appropriate work of the librarian.

This work once well done, the library, if it is to remain stationary, may pass from the hands of the librarian or collector and organizer, to those of the mere custodian or guard, who protects the books from depredation and injury and answers the calls of those who consult them. These are inexpensive labors. One man of common intelligence in a library thus perfectly organized, and receiving no accessions, would be sufficient to take charge of a hundred thousand volumes or more, and serve a large number of readers.

I dwell upon this point, because I think it is not generally understood that the chief expense of a library is in its organization, rather than in its permanent custody. The two things should always be kept distinct. A system for rightly ordering a library should be early formed and steadily adhered to. Sufficient aid of the right kind should be furnished to the librarian, to enable him to incorporate accessions at once among the other portions of the collection; to catalogue them, and render them in the highest degree useful. A collection of books is not all that constitutes a library, any more than a collection of men is of necessity an army. The men must be organized for warlike operations to compose an army; so books, to form a library, must be arranged for purposes of study and reference.

The necessity of the proper management of a library is, however, better appreciated than the labor which it requires.

In nearly all the large libraries of Europe (that of the University of Gottingen is perhaps the only exception) the librarians have not been furnished with the necessary aid to properly dispose of accessions as they were received. The consequence is, that the work of organizing has remained unaccomplished, and that the librarians have been turned into mere custodians, from the impossibility of committing to servants what would otherwise be their work. The books were not so placed that they could be found and kept by mere servitors. The memory and learning of the librarian is in incessant demand from the want of printed guides, which ought to have been provided. Thus arrears have gone on accumulating, and the expenses of the collections have constantly increased.

The view which we take of the necessity of large collections of books leads us to express the gratification which we feel at the large appropriations made this year by Congress for replenishing the desolated shelves of its library. Should this liberality be continued, it will be providing with great rapidity for many of the wants which it has been our purpose to signalize. We doubt whether any appropriation made by Congress has been hailed with more intelligent pleasure. It revived the hopes of the studious throughout the country, and led to the belief that the hands which had begun this good work would carry it on to perfection. With an overflowing treasury, the possession of an enlightened and appreciative nation, we may well hope that money will not be wanting to establish the independence of American learning, to render it no longer provincial, no longer relying for its support upon the libraries of Europe.

•　　•　　•

ON LIBRARIANS AND
CONFERENCES OF LIBRARIANS

In 1853, when Charles B. Norton decided to move to organize the first conference of librarians, he instructed an assistant, Seth Hastings Grant, to write to Jewett soliciting his support and, hopefully, his active involvement in the meeting. Jewett's reply is interesting for a number of reasons.

First, it testifies to his willingness to help in any project that might advance the library profession. He was a generous man who, like all professional leaders, was willing to make great personal sacrifices to serve his profession.

Second, it contains a candid and stinging assessment of the personalities and commitment of many of those who were staffing the nation's libraries.

Finally, it demonstrates that Jewett's own self-image was rather meek and unassuming. However, his definition of the good librarian represents an advance over previous definitions and constitutes a substantial step toward the aggressive and self-confident image projected by Melvil Dewey in the September 30, 1876, *Library Journal*:

> The time has come when a librarian may, without assumption, speak of his occupation as a profession. . . . The best librarians are no longer men of merely negative virtues. They are positive, aggressive characters, standing in the front rank of the educators of their communities. . . . The passive has become active. . . . The Librarian is in the highest sense a teacher. . . . Will any man deny to the high calling of such a librarianship the title of profession?

If librarianship had advanced to such heights by 1876, a portion of the credit must go to Charles Coffin Jewett.

●　　　●　　　●

Source: Charles Coffin Jewett to Seth Hastings Grant. Washington, 16 August 1853. In the Seth Hastings Grant Papers in the American Library Association Archives now deposited in the Archives of the University of Illinois.

My Dear Sir:

I received yesterday your letter of the 13th inst. and hasten to reply. I was very glad to hear from you respecting the librarians' convention, for I have of late felt considerable solicitude about it. Are we likely to have a respectable number present? And will those who come, be prepared to take an active part? We ought, perhaps, before calling the convention to have obtained positive promises from a sufficient number to have rendered it certain that the meeting would be spirited. Since the call was published, I have seen but very few who would be likely to take an interest in the convention. But I have found some, on whom I had counted, who seem unwilling to take any active part. The fact is our fraternity are generally very quiet, unostentatious men, not accustomed to public speaking, or fond of exhibiting themselves. Besides, our pursuits are not of such nature, as to reward our labors by brilliant discourses, or results that will resound in the busy world. We must work hard and long, with small visible effect, and in the track where hundreds, more learned than ourselves perhaps, have worked before us. More than all this, there are but few—very few—who have devoted themselves professionally to bibliography. This taken up by the young man for a few years till he can "get something better to do" or assumed as an extra labor to eke out the income of some half paid professor.

But, notwithstanding all this, there are some among us, who feel a professional interest in the office of librarian; there are private gentlemen too, engrossed in other business it is true, but still finding time for the cultivation of bibliographical pursuits with great success. It is undeniable too that in our civilization, engrafted upon that of the old world and drawing thence and through that its sap, but spreading out into a more luxuriant growth than ever could have been attained by the parent tree, to yield richer and more abundant fruit—books and libraries are to assume and are assuming a new and more important function than ever before. But I need not say all this to you. I allude to it to show my own views respecting the convention, that though we may not be able to do much this year, we are starting in the right direction. The meeting this year cannot be a failure unless we raise expectations which we cannot meet. If but a dozen of us meet round a table to talk together over library economy for a day and concert measures for future meetings—it will be beneficial. But I hope that more can be done. Such things are generally started by a correspondence among those interested in the matter. Each agrees to be present and promises to do his part to make the occasion valuable and spirited. It has not been possible to do this to any great extent in the present case. I do not know how many you may have conferred with, or what may have been promised. I would have made more effort had it been in my power. But my private affairs have taken every moment of time that I could spare from official duties, and the latter have been, on account of the protracted sickness of my first assistant at the time when I most needed him doubly onerous. I cannot do much now. I will (Providence permitting) be present and contribute all that I can. I should like to bring forward, for a full and familiar discussion, my catalogue plan, or rather the "Smithsonian Catalogue System" as I prefer to call it. The second edition of the book which I printed last year is in press and I hope will be completed before the meeting. This much enlarged and I hope improved. I have prepared as examples under the rules, the titles of all the bibliographical works in this Library. To these I hope soon to add those of the Astor Library, Brown University and the Boston Athenaeum, etc., and thus have a complete catalogue of all the bibliographical works in the country. To these I propose hereafter to add notes original and selected.

We are at work on the catalogues of the Library of Congress. Our force is 3 cataloguers, 2 compositors, 1 stereotyper and a boy to assist. The work is going bravely on notwithstanding the sickness of Mr. Corson on whose assistance I had so much relied. I hope to have a considerable number of titles to exhibit. The whole system is now fairly started and I am ready to have it talked about. I particularly wish to have it understood by the librarians. I want them, if they approve of it, to give me their countenance and support, for without them I can do nothing. To this end, I hope to have a familiar discussion, where questions can be asked and doubts and difficulties suggested freely. I will send you the sheets of the books as they are worked off. This edition will be for the public and may therefore be spoken of openly. The last edition I published for private distribution and the criticism of friends.

If thought desirable I will also read an article on the Classification of books. I may also find among my long neglected papers something else which may do to read if it is desirable. But I hope others will occupy the time. I have no time for preparation.

It seems to me very desirable that some arrangements should be made beforehand, to prevent unnecessary delay after we meet. These arrangements can only be made by yourself and others in New York. Is Mr. Cogswell now in the city? Can you not consult with him and Mr. Moore and Mr. Fiske and Mr. Felt—Mr. Putnam perhaps. Mr. Norton will I hope be back in time to help and a most efficient helper he is too. Will Mr. Cogswell be present and will he accept the office of President? Either he or Mr. Folsom ought I think to hold the office. I have thought it might be well to address a circular to those supposed to be most interested in the matter, requesting them to inform you immediately whether they will be present, and also to send to you the title of any article which they may have to present and to name any topic which they would like to introduce for discussion. From the replies we should be able to judge what can be done and can quickly arrange a programme. The nominating committee, etc., can be selected informally the evening of the meeting. Written reports can hardly be expected at this session. The course of business will probably be to listen to such papers as may be offered and then to discuss the subject and if desired pass resolutions, refer to Committees, etc.

It would be very desirable to write to a few gentlemen, such as Mr. Folsom, Mr. Haven, Mr. Herrick, Mr. Livermore, Mr. Hale, etc., asking them to prepare a paper for presentation. I would do this if I could but I do not see how it is possible. The list of topics which you present is a very excellent one. Can you write to these gentlemen and get them to promise the papers. There is one other topic which I should like to bring forward if circumstances favor it—I mean that of a National Library of reference and research. I will write a form of circular which will show my views with reference to it.

You must not think it an assumption on your part to take these preliminary steps. Some one in New York must do it, or the whole thing will be a failure. If you and one or two others in New York will draw up a circular and send it to all librarians and others particularly interested in such matters, I have no doubt it will do more than anything else that can be done to promote the success of the enterprise. You may fall back upon me to any extent to back you up—only "go ahead!"

I have written very hastily and consequently with great prolixity not having time to condense. If anything else occurs to you that you wish to communicate with me about, I shall probably be here till the 14th Sept. and I will endeavor to answer your letters at once.

I remain, Most sincerely yours,

C. C. Jewett

S. H. Grant, Esq., N. Y.

JEWETT'S PRESIDENTIAL ADDRESS

On September 15, 1853, eighty-two librarians and bookmen registered for the first conference of librarians ever held. Among those present were many of the nation's leading librarians, including such men as Charles Folsom, Librarian at the Boston Athenaeum; Lloyd P. Smith, Librarian of the Library Company of Philidelphia; and Charles Coffin Jewett.

Jewett, at 37 years of age, was one of the younger men at the conference but was recognized as the most influential figure present. After ceremoniously offering the Chair to Folsom, who was the Nestor of the group, those present unanimously elected Jewett as their President.

Upon taking the Chair, Jewett addressed the assembly. He spoke eloquently, even fervently, of their purpose for meeting and of their high calling. His speech certainly was appropriate as a keynote address, and it evidenced careful preparation. There is no doubt that it made a lasting impression on those who heard it delivered, and it remains a moving call to professional action.

● ● ●

It must be highly gratifying to those who signed the call for this Convention, to notice the response which it, this morning, receives. To every one who knows the nature of a librarian's duties,—the details which consume his days, and render absence from his post impossible, except at the cost of severe labor on his return,—it must be manifest that we have met at considerable personal sacrifice. We obey some strong and wide-felt impulse in incurring the expense and the trouble of this gathering.

Source: *Norton's Literary and Educational Register for 1854*. The complete Proceedings of the Conference are reproduced in facsimile in George Burwell Utley's *The Librarians' Conference of 1853* (Chicago: American Library Association, 1951).

The call for this Convention was not the result of a correspondence among librarians, nor was it the subject of long and careful consideration. It was, rather, a spontaneous movement. It was first, I think, suggested a year ago, or more, in the Literary Gazette. Librarians spoke to each other on the matter, when they happened to meet. Every one was pleased with the idea. At length a formal call was written, and signed by a few who happened to meet the gentlemen having charge of the paper.

In compliance with such an invitation, we have assembled this morning. It is not, so far as I know, proposed to accomplish any end by this Convention, beyond the general one expressed in the call, of "conferring together upon the means of advancing the prosperity and usefulness of public libraries," and of seeking mutual instruction and encouragement in the discharge of the quiet and unostentatious labors of our vocation, for which each, at his separate post, finds perhaps but little sympathy—for which each, when at home, must derive enthusiasm only from within himself, and from the silent masters of his daily communion.

We have no peculiar views to present, no particular set of measures to propose. We meet without preparation. No order of business has been arranged. Our proceedings must be spontaneous as our meeting. It is not important that they be systematic and formal. We come to receive and to act upon suggestions. We are not here for stately debate, for conspicuous action, much less for an exhibition of ourselves. These things are foreign from our vocation, and not congenial with our tastes. We meet for familiar, informal, conversational conference, where each may take his part, and no one be prevented from contributing his share to the profits of the enterprise, by his inexperience in public speaking, or his inability to make elaborate preparation. Those gentlemen connected with the public press who honor us with their presence, must have been attracted hither by a scholarlike sympathy with our quiet pursuits, which will lead them to appreciate our feelings in this respect, in the reports which they may give.

It is indeed to be hoped that our meeting will have its influence upon the public mind. If our discussions are natural and unrestrained, suggested and shaped by right views of the position which we hold, or ought to hold, in general society and in the republic of letters; if they present to ourselves and to others the difficulties with which we have to contend; if they elicit thought and information upon the collecting of books for private culture, for public enlightenment, and for learned investigations, and upon the best means of promoting the increase and efficiency of such collections;—if we manifest here, while we talk of books as material objects, and of books in their internal significance, that respectful, dignified, and noiseless spirit inspired by the associations in the midst of which we live, the public will certainly feel and acknowledge the beneficial influence of our meeting, and will desire an official report of the progress and results of our deliberations.

The occasion is one of peculiar interest. This is the first convention of the kind, not only in this country, but, so far as I know, in the world.

There have, indeed, been bibliographical associations, but they have been, for the most part, composed of *dilettante*, and not of practical librarians and lovers of books. The gratification of a passion for rare and curious books has generally been their object. Books were too often valuable to them, only as they were worthless to the rest of the world. Each member glorying in the possession of a unique copy of some old work, was required to reprint it, with only copies enough to give one to each member. One society has played the part of *bibliotaph*, by requiring, that if a member dies, and his copy of one of these reprints is to be sold by auction, it shall be bought by the Society at any price it may be necessary to pay.

These associations have had their origin in a different state of society from ours. We can at present have but little sympathy with their principal design. We have none whatever with their selfishness.

We would not be supposed to chide the passion for book rarities, where it exhibits itself simply in collecting and perserving what is curious and costly, and not in its destruction or concealment. Why should not a rich man spend his money in this way, as well as in a thousand others which are harmless? We may go further, and assert that a collection of rare books can scarcely be formed, without subserving the interests of learning, whether made with such a design or not. The public are not unfrequently surprised by results anticipated only by the collector.

I may allude, in this connection, to a distinguished gentlemen in our own country, who made, at great expense, a collection of early-printed books, without any regard to the subjects of which they treated, the languages in which they were written, or their worth as literary productions. By those who did not know his purpose, he was called a *bibliomaniac*. He had, however, a definite object in view, which was, to investigate the early history of typography by its monuments. Books which he never cared to read, were full of instruction to him. He deduced from the close examination of them, many facts new to the bibliographical world, and showed the unsoundness of many generally received theories. For example, he satisfied himself that books, in the early days of typography, were never printed from block letters, that is, from separate types of wood, or of wood faced with metal. He proved, too, that many of these books were printed one page at a time. It had been supposed that the early printers must have had immense fonts of type. In many folios the sheets are quired, and it was very naturally supposed that the type of every page of the quire must have been set up before any was printed off. But he traced a broken letter from page to page, and he found such irregularities of register as could not have occured, had the two pages of the same form been printed at the same time; and he thus demonstrated that these books were printed page by page, and that consequently only a very small font of type was necessary.

Now, these are new, interesting, and valuable results; and they are only specimens which occur to me at the moment, of deductions from the examination of books, which an ordinary observer would say it was infatuation to collect.

But our object, at present, is of a more manifestly and eminently practical and utilitarian character. We meet to provide for the diffusion of a knowledge of good books, and for enlarging the means of public access to them. Our wishes are for the public, not for ourselves.

In our assembling to-day we obey the impulses of our peculiar civilization. We are preeminently a reading people. In Prussia the whole population are taught to read; but a distinguished citizen of that country, who had traveled in the United States, once expressed to me the difference between his own countrymen and the Americans, by saying: "Our people *can* read, your people *do* read." The generally diffused love of reading, for the sake of gaining information, has led to the establishment of a large number of libraries, so that, in the number and general diffusion of small collections of books, we are richer already than any other country in the world. Reading creates the desire to read more, and select reading increases the desire to read profitably. Hence, in every village the questions are asked: "How shall we get good books? How shall we keep them? How shall we use them?" To consult on the best replies to questions like these, is one of the objects of our assembling to-day.

Another demand of our peculiar civilization is, for the means of thorough and independent investigation. We wish to own no men as masters. We intend to re-examine all history from our own American stand point, and we must rewrite it, where we find its facts have been tortured to teach the doctrines of injustice and oppression. The mental activity of this country is surveying every field of research, literary, scientific, aesthetic, industrial, and philanthropic. It requires to know what others have done and thought, that it may itself press farther outward. This country, therefore, demands the means of the amplest research, and this demand must and will be met.

These views have impressed themselves deeply upon our minds, as we are the appointed custodians of the literary treasures of the country, and have led us to desire mutual assistance and concentration of efforts in providing for these intellectual necessities of our American life. For our present meeting it has been proposed to adopt the simplest form of organization; to appoint, besides a president and a secretary, a business committee to receive suggestions and propositions, and arrange the order of proceedings for each day's session. I unite most cordially in the hope which I have heard expressed this morning, that this Convention may be the precursor of a permanent and highly useful association.

THE SMITHSONIAN INSTITUTION
AND ITS PLAN OF CATALOGING

On the morning of the second day of the Librarians' Conference of 1853, Jewett relinquished the Chair to Samuel Foster Haven, Librarian of the American Antiquarian Society, and addressed the conference on the "Smithsonian Cataloguing system."

His speech, at once articulate and carefully organized, was in reality much more than this. Jewett began by outlining the history of the Smithsonian Institution, explaining why the promised book budget never materialized; moved to a justification of his cherished dream for a national library; and finally, turned to an in-depth consideration of his stereotype cataloging plan. His object, as he noted in a letter to Guild, was to gain the endorsement and continued support of the Country's librarians, for without it, he said, "I can do nothing."

That he achieved his objective is readily apparent from a reading of the many flattering and supportive resolutions that were offered by his sympathetic collegues at the conclusion of his address. All in all, this effort represents perhaps his best formal address.

●   ●   ●

It is well known to you, Mr. Chairman, and to other gentlemen present, that previous to the passage of the act of Congress establishing the Smithsonian Institution, various propositions were from time to time made to Congress, for the appropriation of the fund bequeathed to the United States by James Smithson, "to found at Washington an establishment for the increase and diffusion of knowledge among men." One project was to establish an astronomical observatory, another to form an agricultural school, another to found a National University, another to place the money under the charge of the

---

Source: *Norton's Literary and Educational Register for 1854*. The complete Proceedings of the Conference are reproduced in facsimile in George Burwell Utley, *The Librarians' Conference of 1853* (Chicago: American Library Association, 1951).

National Institute, &c, &c. No one of the many plans suggested met the approval of Congress, until Mr. Choate proposed, and in one of his most brilliant and effective speeches advocated, the establishment of a great central library of reference and research. His bill met with general approval and passed the Senate, but was lost among other unfinished business in the lower House. At the next session of Congress, a select committee was appointed by the House of Representatives, upon the administration of the Smithsonian trust. The members of this committee were divided in opinion. They finally reported a bill, in which the Library was a subordinate but still an important feature. When this bill came up for discussion, Mr. Choate's plan was vigorously attacked by one of the leading members of the committee; but it found powerful advocates. Mr. Marsh defended the library in a speech of great learning, ability and eloquence. So strongly did the House approve of Mr. Marsh's views, that when he introduced a series of amendments, designed, as he expressly stated, "to direct the appropriation entirely to the purpose of a library," everything which he proposed was adopted. Congress refused to limit the annual appropriation for the Library to 10,000 or even 20,000 dollars. By fixing the maximum of the annual appropriation at $25,000, a sum nearly equal to the whole income of the fund, Congress unequivocally indicated its intentions, had they not been made sufficiently clear by other votes.

The principal management of the Institution was intrusted to a Board of Regents, composed of three Senators, three Representatives, six citizens of the States, appointed by joint resolution, and three members ex officio, namely, the Vice President of the United States, the Chief Justice of the Supreme Court, and the Mayor of the City of Washington. It was soon found that there were two prominent parties in the Board—not hostile parties, for there is nothing hostile in such matters, but parties of different views in reference to the objects to be pursued by the Institution. One party was in favor of adhering to the library plan, stamped as it was with the approval of Congress; the other was in favor of expending the income in publications and scientific researches. After considerable discussion, it was agreed to divide the income of the Institution permanently between the two great departments: that of collections in literature, science and art, and that of publications and scientific researches.

This plan was followed for a time, but at present a large proportion of the fund is appropriated to other purposes than those of the Library. During the last year only about 1,000 dollars were expended in the purchase of books, and during the present year a still smaller sum will be thus devoted. It has seemed to me my duty to state to you these facts, in order that you might understand the precise position of the Smithsonian Library, the ground of the expectations which had been raised respecting it, and the reasons why they had not been realized. I am happy to add to the statement which I have made, that whatever may have been the feeling with reference to the purchase of books, the "active operations" of the library department—the collection and publication of statistics of libraries, the increase and dissemination of bibliographical knowledge, the development and support of the catalogue system, &c.—have met with cordial approval and support. This must be gratifying to those who hear me. I doubt not that whatever may be the policy of the Institution with reference to its own collections, it will do all that its means will allow for the benefit of other libraries.

For myself I have always believed, and still believe, that a large central library of reference and research will be collected at the Smithsonian Institution, if not by the expenditure of the funds of the Institution, by other means. The funds of the Institution are very small, in comparison with the necessities of literature and science in this country, and when we are obliged to choose among worthy objects, there will be sure to be different opinions. I feel, however, that the formation of the library is a matter sure to be accomplished—if not immediately, yet before many years. A great central library is an important national object; as necessary, to secure the literary independence of this people, as was the war of the Revolution to secure its political independence. It is an object which, besides attracting donations and bequests from the rich, may receive appropriations from our national treasury. Congress, having the control of the treasury of this rich, mighty, and intelligent nation, will not, I believe, be backward in making appropriations for this object, whenever it shall be suitably presented to them. Congress may be regarded as liberal in matters of science and of learning, whenever they are sure that the money will be honestly and properly expended. Many men do not believe this. But look at the action for replenishing the desolated hall of the Library of Congress. Most persons were of opinion that Congress could not be brought to make an appropriation exceeding $30,000 for this purpose; but, when Mr. Chandler proposed $75,000, it was readily granted. It would have been had he asked $200,000, if they had thought that sum necessary, and believed that it would be honestly and judiciously devoted to the gathering of a good library.

There is one other remark I wish to make respecting the position of the Smithsonian Institution among the other literary institutions of the country. So far as I know, it possesses, claims, desires, no authority or power of dictation. The principle has been established and steadily pursued, of occupying, as far as possible, untenanted ground. The position of the Institution at Washington, its connection with the government, and its large fund, devoted by its donor and by the act of Congress to the promotion of the cause of knowledge, give to it the means of doing much which could not otherwise be accomplished for literature and science. In these efforts it needs and relies on the cordial support of other institutions, which, I am happy to say, it has always received. Whenever it is found that any other society or any individual is ready and able to take up and carry out its plans, they are immediately relinquished by us. I may here give one instance, that of Mr. Norton's *Literary Gazette*. Mr. Norton had formed the plan of publishing the Gazette, without knowing that a similar project had been recommended by myself for the bibliographical department of the Smithsonian Bulletin. He proposed to give the bibliographical intelligence in connection with advertisements, which he thought would eventually be profitable to him. When he saw what I had written, he came on to Washington, and offered to abandon his plan. But we were glad to find that he was willing to undertake to accomplish the same purpose which we had in view, and gave up the whole to him, offering him such assistance as we could render, and encouraging him to believe that the enterprise would prove a profitable one. I am happy to know that this expectation has been fully justified; and I hope that the prosperity of this useful journal will continually increase.

In reference to these remarks, Mr. Hayward, of Ohio, presented the following resolution, which was adopted unanimously.

> *Resolved*, That the thanks of this Convention be presented to the Board of Regents and Officers of the Smithsonian Institution, for their steady and effective efforts for the increase and diffusion of knowledge among men, and particularly for the measures which they have adopted for the encouragement and promotion of the public libraries of our country; and we have great pleasure in looking to that institution as the central establishment of the United States for the furtherance of all such objects.

THE SMITHSONIAN CATALOGUE SYSTEM

Prof. Jewett then proceeded to remark:

The catalogue system of which I intend to speak, is one of those enterprises which could not have been carried into operation except under the protection and guidance of the Smithsonian Institution; nor can it be successful, unless it meets the hearty approval and co-operation of other libraries. I wish, therefore, to present the matter fully and explicitly to this Convention.

Few persons, except librarians, are aware of the nature and extent of the difficulties which have been encountered in attempting to furnish suitable printed catalogues of large and growing libraries; difficulties apparently insurmountable, and menacing a common abandonment of the hope of affording guides, so important, to the literary accumulation of the larger libraries of Europe.

While the catalogue of a large library is passing through the press, new books are received, the titles of which it is impossible, in the ordinary manner or printing, to incorporate with the body of the work. Recourse must then be had to a supplement. In no other way can the acquisitions of the library be made known to the public. If the number of supplements be multiplied, as they have been in the library of Congress, the student may be obliged to grope his weary way through ten catalogues, instead of one, in order to ascertain whether the book which he seeks be in the library. He cannot be certain, even then, that the book is not in the collection, for it may have been received since the last appendix was printed. Supplements soon become intolerable. The whole catalogue must then be re-arranged and re-printed. The expense of this process may be borne so long as the library is small, but it soon becomes burdensome, and, ere long, insupportable, even to national establishments.

There is but one course left—not to print at all. To this no scholar consents, except from necessity. But to this alternative, grievous as it is, nearly all the large libraries of Europe have been reluctantly driven.

More than a century has passed, since the printing of the catalogue of the Royal Library at Paris was commenced. It is not yet finished. No one feels in it the interest which he would, if he could hope to have its completeness sustained, when once brought up to a given date.

Not one European library, of the first class, has a complete printed catalogue, in a single work. The Bodleian Library is not an exception. It may be necessary to search six distinct catalogues, in order to ascertain whether any specified book was or was not in that collection, at the close of the year 1847.

This is, surely, a disheartening state of things. It has been felt and lamented by every one who has had the care of an increasing library.

As a remedy for this evil, it is proposed to stereotype the titles separately, and to preserve the plates or blocks, in alphabetical order of the titles, so as to be able readily to insert additional titles, in their proper places, and then to reprint the whole catalogue. By these means, the chief cost of republication (that of composition) together with the trouble of revision and correction of the press, would, except for new titles, be avoided. Some of the great difficulties which have so long oppressed and discouraged librarians, and involved libraries in enormous expenses, may be thus overcome.

The peculiar position of the Smithsonian Institution suggested the application of this plan, on a wider scale, and for a more important purpose, than that of merely facilitating the publication of new and complete editions of separate catalogues.

It had been proposed to form a general catalogue of all the books in the country, with reference to the libraries where each might be found. The plan of stereotyping titles separately, suggested the following system for the accomplishment of this important purpose:

1. The Smithsonian Institution to publish rules for the preparation of Catalogues.

2. Other institutions, intending to publish catalogues of their books, to be requested to prepare them in accordance with these rules, with a view to their being stereotyped under the direction of the Smithsonian Institution.

3. The Smithsonian Institution to pay the whole extra expense of stereotyping, or such part thereof as may be agreed upon.

4. The stereotyped titles to remain the property of the Smithsonian Institution.

5. Every library acceding to this plan, to have the right of using all the titles in the possession of the Institution as often as desired, for the printing of its own catalogue by the Smithsonian Institution, paying only the expense of making up the pages, of press-work, and of distributing the titles to their proper places.

6. The Smithsonian Institution to publish, as soon as possible, and at stated intervals, a General Catalogue of all Libraries coming into this system.

I have already presented to members of the Convention copies of an unfinished work entitled the "Smithsonian Catalogue System." It contains: 1. A detailed account of the system; 2. Rules for the preparation of Catalogues; 3. Examples illustrating the rules. As to the first two matters, the work is complete. It was intended to print as examples the titles of all the works, in the department of bibliography and literary history, in the Smithsonian Library. These titles, to the number of one thousand, are stereotyped and ready for use. The progress of the work was interrupted by the sickness and absence of two of the men on whom we relied. I have been able to print off a few copies, by using the type for the last form of the rules instead of the stereotype plates as in the rest of the book, by limiting the number of examples and omitting the indexes. I hope in a few weeks to be able to finish this book, and to present it through the Smithsonian Institution to the public, as the first detailed publication of the system. About three years ago I read a paper on the subject before the American Scientific Association. I did not present the matter before the public, till the practicability of stereotyping by separate titles had been demonstrated. Practical sterotypers had said that it could not be done. But the perseverance and ingenuity of a gentleman now present, the Rev. Mr. Hale, of Worcester, showed that it could be done by the electrotype process, and even by the common stereotype process. This point once proved, we sought the best method of executing the work. About this time, Mr. Josiah Warren, of Indiana, called our attention to the new process and material for stereotyping which he had patented. We gave them a thorough trial, and at last adopted them. We have done much to perfect the process, and we are now ready to show to experts in practical printing the results which we have attained. The perfecting of this mode of stereotyping, the adaptation of it to our purposes, and the arrangement of the practical details for the great work upon which we are commencing, have consumed much time and demanded great labor. The mechanical difficulties which we have had to meet and overcome will be appreciated by printers and stereotypers. The bibliographical difficulties will be fully understood by librarians. As soon as the practicability of the system had been established, as fully as it could possibly be, before its actual application on a large scale, and the value of it to the world of learning had been considered and proclaimed by a commission of the most competent men to whom the subject was referred by the Smithsonian Institution, the matter was presented to the Joint Library Committee of Congress. They considered it fully, and in the most liberal spirit, and finally recommended to Congress an appropriation for the cataloguing of its library upon this plan. This appropriation was readily granted. It is sufficient to enable us to prosecute the work till next December or January. It is not enough to finish the catalogue, but it is all that was asked for. We wish to proceed cautiously—demonstrating, step by step, the practicability and usefulness of our operations. The work on the catalogue of the Library of Congress is now in progress. The system is therefore in actual operation. . . .

The title of every book and of each distinct edition is stereotyped upon a separate plate. The author's name also stands by itself. Each plate shows at a glance the heading to which it belongs. It is obvious that these plates may be placed together in alphabetical or other order, as may be desired. They are mounted on blocks for printing like other stereotype plates. The great ends to be gained are:

1. To avoid the necessity of preparing, composing, and correcting anew the titles once printed, when the Library has received accessions, or the alternative of printing the titles of these accessions in supplements, which are very inconvenient appendages.

2. To prevent the repetition of the work of preparation of titles, composition and correction of press, for copies of the same book in different libraries. The title once prepared and stereotyped, remains at the Smithsonian Institution, to be used by any Library having the same book.

3. To secure uniformity in the construction of catalogues, thus greatly facilitating the researches of the student.

It is obvious that the cost of the first catalogue will be greater than if it were not stereotyped. The work of preparation will also be more expensive. But the additional cost of the first edition will be more than saved in the first reprinting of the whole catalogue. It will be further understood that the sum paid by the first Library is not only for its own benefit, but for that of every other Library hereafter adopting the plan, so far as its books are the same. Congress is therefore now conferring a great boon upon other Libraries, while at the same time it is taking the course, in the end most economical, for the construction of the catalogues of its own Library. There will also be a great saving of the expense of paper and press-work under this system. It is customary now to print off a larger number of copies of every catalogue than are immediately wanted, because it cannot be known how many may be required before the catalogue can be reprinted. On this plan, when a new edition, with all additions incorporated can be had at any time, it will not be thought necessary to print more copies than enough to meet the immediate demand.

It should be mentioned as one of the most important advantages of this system, that it affords the means of attaining great accuracy in the catalogues. Every effort will be made to secure accuracy in the first instance. Librarians will not, however, be surprised to find numerous errors. This system offers the best means of detecting and correcting these errors. Every time that a title is used for a new catalogue, it must be very carefully compared with the book itself. Every mistake and variation will be reported in a friendly spirit, and immediately corrected. The catalogue will thus be constantly undergoing a process of verification and improvement.

Upon all these topics I have dwelt more fully and systematically in the pamphlet to which I have alluded. It may not be amiss for me to notice one or two objections which may occur to the minds of practical printers against the use of these stereotype plates. One is, that the plates, being used so often, will become worn, and that when new plates are inserted, the difference between the new and old plates will be observable on the printed sheets.

To this objection I can say in reply: First, the number of copies required for each catalogue would be so small that it would be many years before there would be any noticeable difference between the old and new plates, were they made from common type metal. But, secondly, the material which we employ is harder than type metal, and resists much longer the wear of the press. I presume that a run of 100,000 copies would not make any observable difference between the old plates and the new.

Another difficulty which may suggest itself to some, is in keeping the register and preserving a uniform length of pages. The register, so far as the top and sides of the page are concerned, can be kept most perfectly. Variations in the length of the pages cannot be entirely avoided. But if some pages be longer or shorter by three or four lines, it is not a very serious matter. It may offend a printer's eye, but would not be noticed by the general reader. I may remark, however, that there are several ways of reducing the inequalities. Very long titles may be stereotyped in two or three pieces. The titles on a short page may be spread apart, making the matter a little more open and thus elongating the page. The catalogue may be printed in double-column folio. This size is preferable for a catalogue on other accounts. It presents more titles to the eye at once, and it also saves paper.

I would not be understood as insisting upon the catalogue being in folio, nor, indeed, upon its being alphabetical. These are matters not essential to the system. Each librarian can choose for himself; the system possessing this great advantage, that it is equally applicable to the folio, quarto, or octavo size; to alphabetical and to classed catalogues.

There is one other point which may be noticed. This kind of catalogue is not recommended for all purposes for which a catalogue or list of books may be desirable. It is proposed as the standard catalogue for reference in every library containing works of permanent value. It is proposed as the basis for all other apparatus, such as indexes, shelf-lists, "finding catalogues," or short title catalogues, which it may be thought that the peculiar circumstances of any library or every library require. From this catalogue all others may easily be made. This is supposed to be, in general, the first and most important of all the means for rendering a library serviceable to all classes of persons who may consult it.

With respect to the rules for preparing catalogues, it may be proper to make a few explanatory remarks. They were formed after a careful study of those adopted for the preparation of the catalogue of the British Museum. They were examined and discussed in detail by the catalogue commission appointed by the Smithsonian Institution. They have been carefully revised to meet exigencies which have occurred in the practical application of them. That they are perfect and all-sufficient, is not, indeed, to be supposed. On many points there would be a difference of opinion. An effort has been earnestly and honestly made to frame the best possible code. But whether it be absolutely the best or not, the great desideratum of uniformity will be attained by the adoption of it.

The practical operation of the rules has been considered, no less than the theoretical perfection of the catalogue. It is necessary to frame such rules as we may reasonably expect to be able to follow. I would gladly have required that the number of pages of every book (distinguishing those of prefatory and appended matter,) and the names of publishers should in all cases be given. But these would require much additional time and labor, and would considerably increase the bulk of the catalogue. It was thought best, therefore, to omit them. We must endeavor to make the catalogue accurate so far as it goes. The examination of the book should be thorough. Additional particulars may hereafter be added in the form of notes, without disturbing the work first done.

The work upon which we have entered is not the work of a day, nor of a year. It demands long-continued, patient labor. Should it be successful, as we have every reason to hope that it will be, its best results will be realized after we have ceased from our labors. But its immediate results will amply reward our efforts. Some of them are now almost attained. The catalogue of the Library of Congress will, it is hoped, be a valuable gift to the bibliographical world. To the list now nearly ready for publication, of the books in the department of bibliography and literary history, belonging to the Smithsonian Library, it will be easy to add those in other libraries not already catalogued. We can then present to librarians a complete catalogue of the bibliographical apparatus to be found in the country. Catalogues of books in other branches of knowledge are now in preparation. As we thus proceed from library to library, and from one department of learning to another, each work will be complete and useful in itself, while it constitutes a finished portion of the general catalogue.

At the conclusion of these remarks, Mr. Folsom presented the following resolutions:—

> *Resolved*, That we have considered attentively the plan for constructing catalogues of libraries, and a general catalogue of the public libraries of the United States, by means of stereotype titles, proposed and developed by the Smithsonian Institution. That we regard it as an object of high importance to the interests of our public libraries, and to the promotion of learning, and worthy to share in the funds of the Institution, and the zealous exertions of its officers; the more so as it is an enterprise which cannot be successfully prosecuted except under the protection, guidance, and pecuniary support of this central establishment, for the increase and diffusion of knowledge.

> *Resolved*, That we have learned with pleasure that Congress, on the recommendation of the Library Committee, made an appropriation for the practical testing of the plan in its application to the Library of Congress, and that the work is now in successful progress.

> *Resolved*, That, as practical librarians and bibliographers, we take pride and satisfaction in the fact that a measure of so great literary utility has received the prompt and efficient support of our national legislature, and we would express the earnest hope that this support be extended to it liberally till its first great result, in the complete stereotyped catalogue of the Library of Congress, shall be attained.

Mr. Smith, of Philadelphia, said he had investigated· Prof. Jewett's plan with considerable interest, and could heartily favor the resolutions. He thought the catalogue of the British Museum even might be completed, and thereby the scholars of the world be greatly benefited, by following this system. He thought the result of this experiment would be one grand catalogue of all the libraries of the United States.

Mr. Haven, of Worcester, said he thought the resolutions should contain some intimation that the idea was purely American in its inception and perfection.

Mr. Folsom said the intent of the resolutions was to stamp it as American.

The propriety of stating more clearly the fact, that the invention of separate stereotyped titles was purely American, was advocated by Mr. Haven, Prof. Greene, and others.

PROF. JEWETT said that within the last few months he had heard that a claim for this invention had been set up in France, by the Chevalier de la Garde, an employee of the National Library. After the speech he [Mr. J.] delivered before the American Scientific Association, M. de la Garde published a letter in the *Moniteur*, in which he stated that he had formed a similar plan eighteen years previous, that he had published an account of it in 1845, and that he had endeavored to secure its adoption. The plan of the Chevalier de la Garde differed in many respects from his own, but still it contained the idea of separate stereotype titles. Mr. J. stated still further, that this claim was entirely unknown to him until long after he had fully matured and had proposed his own system. He had never heard of such a proposition from any source, till after he had suggested it. He certainly hoped that full justice would be done to any earlier efforts than his own which may have been made in this direction.

Mr. HAVEN remarked, that in every great discovery there was always found a number of men who laid claim to be the originators, but it was universally admitted that he who carried a discovery to its successful application was the one entitled to the credit as inventor.

Mr. FOLSOM said that the same idea had struck him thirty years ago, and therefore he had a better claim than the French gentleman. Neither claim amounted to anything. The idea had produced nothing practical and useful. He would say, however, that though he had had the idea, when Prof. Jewett mentioned it to him he said that its practical development was "impossible."

Mr. GUILD, of Providence, said he had at first entertained serious doubts as to the practicability of the system. Those doubts were now entirely removed, and he hoped the time would soon come when every library in the land would have its catalogue made out by means of separate stereotyped titles.

The first resolution was then amended as follows:

Resolved, That we have considered attentively the plan for constructing catalogues of libraries, and a general catalogue of the public libraries of the United States, by means of separate stereotype titles, *originated and* proposed *by Prof. C. C. Jewett*, and developed by *him while librarian of* the Smithsonian Institution, etc.

The three resolutions, as thus amended, were then unanimously adopted. Mr. VINTON, of St. Louis, then presented the following:

Resolved, That a Committee of three be appointed by this Convention, to prepare a history of the invention of applying movable stereotype plates to the printing of the separate titles in a catalogue; and that their report be embodied in a written memorial, to be presented at the next annual session of this Convention, in order that it may be printed at the expense of the Convention.

The resolution was carried unanimously—and Mr. Folsom, of Boston, Mr. Guild, of Providence, and Rev. Mr. Hale, of Worcester, were appointed that Committee.

CENTRAL NATIONAL LIBRARY

Mr. FOLSOM offered the following resolutions, which were adopted unanimously:

Resolved, That the establishment of a great central library for reference and research while it is demanded by the condition of the United States as to general civilization and intellectual advancement, is especially interesting to this Convention from the bearing it would have upon libraries throughout the country.

Resolved, That we deem such an establishment as being eminently worthy of support from the national treasury, and that in no way can the government better promote the progress of learning through the whole country, than by placing a central national library under the administration of the Smithsonian Institution.

ON THE CONSTRUCTION
OF CATALOGUES

Jewett's most famous work, *On the Construction of Catalogues of Libraries*, was an outgrowth of efforts first initiated in 1847. Determined to go ahead with his stereotype catalog idea, he quickly realized that he would have to provide for some means of insuring the uniformity of cataloging copy to be used in his national union catalog. As a result, he promulgated his *Rules for Preparing Catalogues*. When he published his *On the Construction of Catalogues*, it was divided into two parts: (1) a lengthy description of the history, present status, and technical aspects of his stereotype catalog plan, and (2) his *Rules*. While the stereotype scheme was very exciting to his contemporaries, the *Rules* proved the most enduring and influential of Jewett's works.

Since its publication, *On the Construction of Catalogues* has been consistently cited by authors in the areas of cataloging and classification, and, in the opinion of experts in the field, it must be viewed as a "super-classic." Librarians reading Jewett's *Rules* today will find them crude and occasionally inconsistent, but will also note many provocative and useful guidelines. The temptation is to provide a lengthy exegesis of Jewett's work, analyzing its strengths and weaknesses. However, Jewett was an articulate and careful writer—his work needs little introduction—and what he wrote is neither confusing or difficult. Modern-day catalogers will have little difficulty following Jewett's line of reasoning, and will quickly see the strengths and weaknesses of his *Rules*.

In his own time the *Rules* were the basic guide to cataloging practice and remained so until the ascendancy of Cutter and Dewey in the 1870's. Jewett's preeminence is fittingly acknowledged by the leading expert on the catalogs of this period, Jim Ranz, who labeled the third quarter of the nineteenth century as the "Age of Jewett."

Jewett's *Rules* are reprinted in full here, prefaced with a selection of his remarks on the intellectual aspects of catalog production.

● ● ●

Source: *On the Construction of Catalogues of Libraries, and Their Publication by Means of Separate, Stereotyped Titles. With Rules and Examples*. Second Edition. (Washington: Published by the Smithsonian Institution, 1853).

DISTINCTION BETWEEN A CATALOGUE AND A
BIBLIOGRAPHICAL DICTIONARY

A catalogue of a library is, strictly speaking, but a list of the titles of the books, which it contains. It is not generally expected to give any further description of a book than the author gives, or ought to give in the title-page, and the publisher, in the imprint, or colophon; except the designation of form, which is, almost universally, added.

A bibliographical dictionary is supposed to contain, besides the titles of books, such descriptions, more or less extended, drawn from all available sources of information, as may be necessary to furnish means of identifying each work, of distinguishing its different editions, of ascertaining the requisites of a perfect copy, of learning all facts of interest respecting its authorship, publication, typography, subsequent casualties, alterations, etc., its market value, and the estimation in which it is held.

A catalogue is designed to show what books are contained in a particular collection, and nothing more. Persons in want of further information, are expected to seek for it in bibliographical dictionaries, literary histories, or similar works.

Inasmuch, however, as bibliographical works are not always accessible, or known to the investigator, additions are, not infrequently, made to the titles, in catalogues, of such notices as belong more appropriately to bibliographical dictionaries, ... These, of course, impart to such catalogues greater value and usefulness.

As bibliographers, we cannot indeed but wish, that the catalogue of every library were a bibliographical dictionary of its books.

THE SAME TITLES FOR ALL CATALOGUES

Practically, however, we must restrict our efforts, within the limits of probable accomplishment. There is no species of literary labor so arduous, or which makes so extensive demands upon the learning of the author, as that of the preparation of such works. The most which one man can hope to effect, in this department, is to examine and describe books, in some special branch of knowledge, or books of some particular class, as *palocotypes*, books privately printed, a selection of books most esteemed by collectors, etc. It is too much to expect, that every librarian can find time, or possess learning, for such a description of all books under his care. Besides, this would be a waste of labor and of money. The same description would be prepared and printed, a hundred or a thousand times.

It is doubtless desirable, that such results of *original* investigations of librarians, as are not to be found in any of the bibliographical dictionaries, should be given, in the catalogues which they publish. In other cases, also, as will appear hereafter, it may be important to give, in a catalogue, fuller and more accurate descriptions of books, than are to be found upon their title-pages; but the principle should be established, and ever borne in mind, that a catalogue, being designed to be merely a list of titles, with imprints and designations of size, all additional descriptions should be limited and regulated by explicit rules, in order to give uniformity and system to the work, and to restrict its bulk and cost, within reasonable bounds.

FORM OF THE CATALOGUE

The titles constituting the catalogue may be variously arranged. They may be placed under the names of authors, and the names disposed in alphabetical order; they may be grouped in classes, according to subjects; or they may be made to follow the order of the date, or place of printing.

The two most common forms for catalogues, are the alphabetical and the classed. Much controversy has arisen respecting their comparative usefulness. It is not necessary to revive it here, since the system now proposed, renders it easy to vary the order of titles, so as to suit any desired form.

For the General Catalogue, however, it is, for several reasons, desirable to adopt the alphabetical arrangement.

It would be impossible to propose any system of classification, which would command general approval, or upon which a commission of competent bibliographers would be unanimous in opinion. A classification, founded upon the nature of things, though it has occupied the best thoughts of such men as Bacon, Leibnitz, D'Alembert, Coleridge, Ampère, and many others, has not yet been attained. Every classification which has been proposed or used, is more or less arbitrary, and consequently unsatisfactory, and liable to be altered or superseded.

If, however, it were possible to agree upon a system of classification, the attempt to carry it out would, in a work like that proposed, be fatal to uniformity. Where different men were applying the same system, their opinions would vary, with their varying intelligence and skill. This would lead to utter and irremediable confusion, and would eventually defeat all our plans.

Even were these objections obviated, the occurrence of fewer difficulties in constructing an alphabetical catalogue would still present a decisive argument in its favor. Even these are great. If increased, by an attempt at classification, they would soon lead to an abandonment of the work.

Another consideration of great weight is, that, in reprinting classified catalogues, and inserting additions, if the titles were kept in systematic order, the work of selecting those to be used, and of distributing them to their places, would have to be done by a person, who, besides being a practical printer, should be familiar with the bibliographical system adopted. This would be very expensive. Whereas, on the alphabetical plan, any printer could do the whole.

On general considerations, without special reference to those which are peculiar to this system of publishing, alphabetical catalogues are to be preferred;—catalogues in which all the works of each author are placed under his name, and the names of authors are arranged alphabetically; anonymous works being entered under the first word of the title, not an article or preposition. Such is now the general opinion of competent bibliographers and literary men.

The Edinburgh Review, in an able and interesting article upon the British Museum, holds the following language:

"It seems to have been almost universally agreed that the catalogue ought to be alphabetical. Some time ago the current of opinion among literary men seemed to be setting towards classed catalogues, or those in which the books are arranged according to subjects. We had hardly supposed that this illusion (as we hold it to be) had become so nearly obsolete as the evidence before us shows that it is: and this disappearance of a most injurious opinion, which never was entertained to any extent by the really experienced in bibliography, encourages us to hope that it will not be long before the *professional* persons just alluded to (librarians) will be admitted to know best on all the points which have been raised relative to the care of a large library."

The experience of all students, of all who use books, if carefully noted, will show, that, in a vast majority of cases, whoever wishes to refer to books in a library, knows the names of their authors. It follows, that this form of arrangement must be, in the main, the most convenient; and if any other be pursued, it can but accommodate the minority, at the expense of the majority.

Still, it is indisputable that, oftentimes, the names of authors are not known; that one knows, merely, what subjects he wishes to investigate.

It may be said, that a catalogue, being designed to be merely a list of books contained in a library, is not to be expected to furnish this information; and that references to all authors, treating of any particular subjects, may be obtained from bibliographical works, encyclopaedias, and other sources of information. This is true. But, unfortunately, these sources of information are not generally known, or not readily accessible, even to men of considerable attainments and scholarship.

It becomes, then, a question of importance how far the wants of such persons are to be provided for.

•   •   •

But it is convenient even for those to whom the principles and means of research are best known, to be able to ascertain, readily, what books, of those which they know to have been written upon the subjects of their investigation, are to be found in the particular libraries which they consult. This end may be attained in the following manner. In connection with the *catalogue* of each library, there should be an *index* of subjects. This index should also be alphabetical. Under each subject, the divisions which naturally belong to it, should be distinctly recognized. It may here be remarked, that the parts of any particular science, or branch of learning, may be clearly defined, and universally acknowledged, whilst the relation of this science, or branch of learning, to others, may not be clearly established.

•   •   •

This index should be alphabetical, rather than classed, because it is easier to find a word, in an alphabetical arrangement, than in any other order of classification; and, besides, the subject of research may be one not admitted, as a distinct division, in any classification. Such indexes can hardly be expected, immediately, in connection with the general catalogue; though, it is to be hoped, that these valuable appendages will not long be, of necessity, omitted.

A method of securing uniformity in such indexes may, hereafter, be agreed upon, so that they may be combined and form an alphabetical index of subjects to the general catalogue. It is thought best, however, for the present, to limit our efforts to the procuring of good alphabetical catalogues, as a groundwork, to which other valuable aids to research, may, as opportunities offer, be superadded.

NECESSITY OF RULES FOR THE PREPARATION
OF CATALOGUES

The preparation of a catalogue may seem a light task, to the inexperienced, and to those who are unacquainted with the requirements of the learned world, respecting such works. In truth, however, there is no species of literary labor so arduous and perplexing. The peculiarities of titles are, like the idiosyncracies of authors, innumerable. Books are in all languages, and treat of subjects as multitudinous as the topics of human thought.

Liability to error and to confusion is, here, so great and so continual, that it is impossible to labor successfully, without a rigid adherence to rules. Although such rules be not formally enunciated, they must exist in the mind of the cataloguer, and guide him, or the result of his labors will be mortifying and unprofitable.

In this country, he who undertakes to prepare a catalogue, goes to the work under great disadvantages, in many respects. Few have had opportunity to acquire the requisite bibliographical knowledge and experience; and few libraries contain the necessary books of reference. A set of rules, therefore, seems peculiarly necessary for the assistance of librarians.

Minute and stringent rules become absolutely indispensable, when the catalogue of each library is, as upon the proposed plan, to form part of a general catalogue. *Uniformity* is, then, imperative; but, among many laborers, can only be secured by the adherence of all to rules embracing, as far as possible, the minutest details of the work.

The rules which follow were drawn up with great care. They are founded upon those adopted for the compilation of the catalogue of the British Museum; some of them are, *verbatim*, the same. Others conform more to rules advocated by Mr. Panizzi, than to those finally sanctioned by the Trustees of the Museum. Many modifications and additions have been made, adapted to the peculiar character of the system now proposed. Some innovations have been introduced, which, it is hoped, may be considered improvements. The commissioners, appointed to examine and report upon the catalogue project, considered not only its general features, but, also, its minute details. To them, were submitted the rules for cataloguing, which were separately discussed, and, after having been variously amended and modified, were recommended for adoption.

It is too much to suppose that any code should provide for every case of difficulty which may occur. The great aim, here, has been to establish principles, and to furnish analogies, by which many cases, not immediately discussed, may be indirectly settled; and, it is believed, that the instances will be few, which cannot be determined, by studying the rules, with the remarks under them, and carefully considering the characteristics of this kind of catalogue.

It should be remembered that a principal object of the rules is to secure *uniformity*; and that, consequently, some rules, which may seem unnecessarily burdensome, and, in certain applications, even capricious, are, all things considered, the best; because they secure that uniformity, which is not otherwise possible of attainment, and without which, the catalogues could not be comprehended in a general system.

DUTIES OF COLLABORATORS AND SUPERINTENDENT

The catalogue of each library is to be prepared, in accordance with the rules, under the immediate direction of the librarian, by transcribers employed by him. Should the system here proposed come into general use, it will probably be found expedient to have persons specially trained to the business, who shall go from place to place, for the purpose of making catalogues. Much of the value of the work will, of course, depend upon the faithfulness and learning of those who first prepare the titles. The qualifications, both natural and acquired, demanded for the suitable accomplishment of their task, are, unfortunately, rare. No person, who is impatient, indolent, inaccurate, or careless in his personal habits; who is ignorant of literary history and bibliography; who is unacquainted with the classical, and with the most important modern languages; or who is destitute of that general knowledge of the circle of the sciences, which is attained in, what is usually called, a liberal education; can be expected to make a catalogue of a general library, that will not be discreditable to the compiler, and to the institution employing him. Great care should, therefore, be exercised in selecting men for such work.

It is proper to remark, in this place, that no one, whatever may be his talents, attainments and industry, can safely work with the rapidity, which the public, and committees (inexperienced in catalogue-making, however judicious and well-instructed in other matters) frequently require. It is impossible to say what would be a good average rate of performance, in cataloguing a library, without knowing exactly the kind of works it contains. The best and only satisfactory criterion is furnished by the rate of progress in the British Museum, the National Library of Paris, and other large libraries containing books of all kinds. A trial of many years has shown that men possessed of the best qualifications, long practised in the work, with every advantage of a systematic division of labor, of access to all necessary books of reference, and to persons who could help them in emergencies, provided with every mechanical facility and assistance to be desired, can prepare about forty or fifty titles a day.

The danger of working with too great rapidity, without rules, and without suitable bibliographical preparation, was most strikingly illustrated during the discussions of the British Museum Commission.

• • •

But the most elaborately formed rules for cataloguing are inadequate to provide for all cases. Doubts and difficulties will unavoidably arise, as to their application. For example, in abridging titles, scarcely any two men would agree, even within the limits of the rules given. It is necessary, therefore, that there should be a central superintendence of the whole enterprise; and that the duties of those who are engaged in preparing the titles, and of the superintendent should be distinctly understood. This object has been kept in view in preparing the rules. The transcribers are to be responsible for exactness, in writing off titles without abridgment; and for a clear statement, in notes, of all peculiarities not mentioned in the titles. They should also indicate the parts of the titles which they think might be omitted.

The titles are then to be submitted to the superintendent. He is to examine them, in order to see that all the rules have been observed. He is to decide upon all abridgments and additions, and mark the manuscript for the printer. He is also to examine the last revise.

• • •

RULES FOR PREPARING CATALOGUES

TITLES

I. The Titles are to be transcribed IN FULL, including the names of Authors, Editors, Translators, Commentators, Continuators, &c., precisely as they stand upon the title-page.

EXCEPTIONS. There are many titles from which much may well be omitted. But to make omissions without prejudice to ready investigation is an extremely difficult and delicate task, in the performance of which, uniformity is highly important; it is therefore desirable that all abridgments be made by the same person. To this end, the rule should stand without exception, so far as the writing out of the titles is concerned. The abridgments for printing should all be made by the superintendent, and only in the following cases:

Additions to names of authors, &c., not necessary for their identification; mottoes, repetitions, or expletives not essential to a full and clear titular description of the book, may be omitted. Omissions of mottoes and devices are to be denoted by three stars; of other matter, by three dots, placed thus . . .

No omission is to be made which requires any change in, or addition to, the phraseology of that part of the title which is retained. Not even an improvement of the title, by any change, is to be allowed.

REMARK 1. This rule is understood to apply only to the principal entry. It is supposed that each title will be entered in full only once. All other entries will refer to this full entry. They will be called *Cross-References*; and rules for their preparation are given hereafter.

REMARK 2. It is necessary (in this plan) to give the name of the Author, in connection with the title, although it be but a repetition of the heading; for the heading will be stereotyped separate from the title, and, therefore, the title should contain all that is necessary to indicate its proper position, in the alphabetical order, in case of displacement.

REMARK 3. Experience shows that it takes less time to transcribe titles in full, than to abridge them with any tolerable degree of accuracy. It requires, too, less learning and experience in the cataloguer. That a catalogue can be made more rapidly, more economically, and more satisfactorily by transcribing the titles faithfully and fully, without the omission of a single letter or point, than by any proper plan of abridgment, cannot be denied by any one who has fairly tried the experiment.* If the catalogue were not to be printed, this rule should have no exception whatever. The printing, however, introduces two considerations to modify the rule, namely, the *expense* of printing, and the *bulk* of the catalogue. The force of the former consideration is much diminished by the plan of stereotyping the titles. It is but a first expense that we have to meet, not a repetition of it. Besides, no library but the first has to print all its titles. The saving, even to the second library, by the use of those already stereotyped, would doubtless far more than counterbalance the extra expense of printing long titles. The bulk of the catalogue is certainly a matter of considerable importance, though of less than might, at first, be supposed. It does not make much difference, in convenience of use, whether such a work as an Encyclopaedia be in a hundred volumes or in ten, though it is, of course, more convenient to refer to one volume than to ten. The proposed general catalogue would doubtless exceed one volume, even with short titles. But convenience should not be allowed to have more influence than the demands of learned investigators. The bulk of catalogues should not be considered in opposition to their accuracy, and to such a degree of fulness of title, as may be necessary to identify the book, and to give all such particulars of information, as may justly be expected from a titular description.

REMARK 4. It is deemed unnecessary to prescribe any particular form of card or paper for use in copying the titles. If they are to be printed at once, it will be found most convenient to write them on one side only of common foolscap paper. Cross references should immediately follow the titles to which they belong. If cards have already been adopted in the library to be catalogued, their form need not be changed. They may be placed in the hands of the printer without being transcribed. A manuscript catalogue for constant use should generally be upon cards. A very convenient method of keeping them is that employed by Mr. Folsom in the Boston Athenaeum. The cards are long and narrow; are so perforated that they may be strung upon cords, which, being elastic, allow free motion without displacement; and are kept in cases, made to resemble folio volumes, one side of which opens like the cover of a book.

---

*A very complete discussion of the comparative advantages of long and short titles is contained in the Report of the Commissioners on the British Museum, with Minutes of Evidence, 1850, particularly in Mr. Panizzi's Letter to the Earl of Ellesmere, in Appendix No. 12.

II. The Titles are to be transcribed WITH EXACTNESS.

REMARK 1. The titles are *not to be translated* by the cataloguer. If, however, the original title, being in a language which does not admit of being represented in the Roman character, be accompanied by a translation into a language for which the Roman alphabet may be used, the latter may be given without the former; this peculiarity being mentioned, with such explanations as will prevent mistake as to the language in which the book is printed. If the book be in several languages, and be provided with title-pages for each, or for several, the cataloguer may give the preference to languages using the Roman alphabet in the following order: English, Latin, French, Italian, Spanish, German. The other title-pages should however be mentioned.

REMARK 2. The *precise phraseology*, however quaint, awkward, or ungrammatical, must be scrupulously followed. When striking faults or errors occur, the cataloguer should write [*sic*], after each of them, to denote that the title has been faithfully copied, and that the error is not attributable to his carelessness.

REMARK 3. The exact mode of *spelling*, however inaccurate or antiquated, must be conscientiously copied. When abbreviations appear upon the title-page, they should, in transcribing, be copied accurately. They should also, if possible, be printed. These are most frequent in early printed Latin and Greek books. If types cannot be had for printing these abbreviations, the word should be given in full; the added letters being italics.

REMARK 4. The *punctuation* of the title-page should also be retained. Sometimes, in the titles of modern books, no pointing is used; in such cases, none should be introduced. Wide spaces may be used instead.

REMARK 5. The *accentuation* of the original should be preserved. In French books, however, it often happens that parts of the title-page are printed in capitals without accents, and other parts in "lower-case" letters with accents. This is attributable to the general want of accents upon what are called "title-letters." To avoid the striking incongruity which would be occasioned by printing one part with, and another without accents, when the same letter is used throughout the title, it will be proper to add the accents, where they are omitted in the titles of foreign books; but not to omit or alter any which occur.

REMARK 6. When possible, the *form of letter* (as Black Letter, Italic, Greek, Hebrew, &c.), is to be preserved. When Black Letter, Italic, or any peculiar letter or cut of type is used, in the title, merely as a typographical embellishment, it is not to be copied; but only when the whole book is printed in it. This rule has no limitation, except the knowledge of the cataloguer, and the means of the printing office. With reference to those languages in which is embodied the great mass of literature, there will be little difficulty in finding men to copy the titles with accuracy; and the printing office should contain varieties of type, Roman, Black Letter, German, Greek, Hebrew, and, in time, fonts of other alphabets.

Books in languages which cannot, at first, be correctly printed or written, should be reported from each library, as accurately and fully as possible. An arrangement may hereafter be made to employ competent persons to catalogue such works, and means may be procured for printing or engraving their titles. No title, however, should be stereotyped for the General Catalogue, till its accuracy and conformity to the rules are fully ascertained.

REMARK 7. This principle does not apply to the *use of capitals or small letters*. Most title-pages are printed wholly in large letters; some are partly in large and partly in small letters. For the catalogue, they are to be written and printed in small letters.

REMARK 8. *Initial capitals* are to be used only when the laws of the language now require them. In English, the first word of every sentence, proper names, adjectives derived from proper names, names of the Deity, the first word of the title of a book quoted within another title, and titles of respect or office, such as Hon., Mr., Dr., Capt., Rev., (whether contracted or not,) prefixed to a name, should be written and printed with initial capitals. In German and Danish, every noun begins with a capital. In French, Spanish, Italian and Portuguese, adjectives derived from proper names, are not, as in English, generally printed with initial capitals. In Latin, the English usage in this particular should be followed. It would doubtless be more satisfactory to make the titles, as printed in the catalogue, perfect transcripts of the title-pages, in respect to the use of initial capitals; but this is hardly practicable. The use of both upper-case and lower-case letters in a title-page, is for the most part a matter of the printer's taste, and does not generally indicate the author's purpose. To copy them in a catalogue with literal exactness would be exceedingly difficult, and of no practical benefit. In those parts of the title-page which are printed wholly in capitals, initials are undistinguished. It would be unsightly and undesirable to distinguish the initials where the printer had done so, and omit them where he had used a form of letter, which prohibited his distinguishing them. It would teach nothing to copy from the book the initial capitals in one part of the title, and allow the cataloguer to supply them in other parts. The only practicable method of securing uniformity or convenience would seem to be, to require, as is done above, the cataloguer to employ initial capitals according to established laws, regardless of the title-page.

There are certain features of title-pages which it is wholly impracticable to transfer to a catalogue. For example, they generally are (as they always should be) *inscriptions*, and as such are meant to have a certain *local disposition* of parts which serves to interpret them, by showing at a glance their relations to each other. A title in a catalogue cannot be expected to retain this important feature of an inscription.

III. The whole Title is to be repeated for every distinct edition of the work; and the number of the edition, if not the first, is to be always given.

REMARK 1. The necessity of this rule arises from the stereotyping of the titles separately. It is frequently the case, that publishers, after having stereotyped a book, call every thousand copies of it a separate edition, and, for twenty or more editions, there may be no alteration in the book, except in the word expressing the number of the edition, and in the date. In such cases, it cannot be necessary to print a separate title for each pretended edition. If there be any important alteration of the book, it should be designated as a distinct edition. This irregularity is found mostly, if not exclusively, in American books, and occurs principally in school-books.

It is easy to see how this artifice of bibliopoles would occasion great trouble to cataloguers, if it were common. Some publishers have introduced the terms "second thousand," "tenth thousand," &c., instead of "second edition," "tenth edition." This is more honest, and for our purposes more convenient. But it is not necessary to introduce these chiliads into the catalogue.

Minor changes are sometimes made in the stereotype plates, after a part of the copies have been printed; that is, some error may be discovered and corrected, or some word substituted for another. But such changes are generally slight and unimportant. They can only be detected by comparing one copy of a book with another, and, when known, are seldom worthy of notice.

Sometimes, the title of a book is the same in two editions, while the body of the work is more or less altered. Sometimes, also, the title is changed while the book remains entirely unaltered. Such instances are, however, of comparatively rare occurrence. They are, or should be, noted in bibliographical dictionaries. It is not often the case, that the two editions are to be found in one library; consequently, an account of such variations cannot be expected from the cataloguer. But, if such facts become known to him, they should be carefully noted.

The increase of the bulk of the catalogue, which this rule will occasion, may appear, at first sight, to be a grave difficulty. It should be considered, however, that the number of books, which reach a second edition, is comparatively small; and, that, although there may be a hundred editions of a book, those only will have their titles repeated, which belong to the library to be catalogued. The increase in bulk will be much less considerable than might be apprehended, and it will be more than compensated for, by the greater exactness of the descriptions. Any one, who has had much experience in examining catalogues, must have been frequently puzzled to ascertain the exact character of several editions of a book, where the only description of any edition after the first, is *"The same,"* or *"Ditto,"* with a different date. We may wish to know whether the titles are identical. In the title of a later edition, some particular may have been given, which to us is very important, but which the cataloguer has omitted. To bibliographers, and men of habits of careful investigation, different editions are different books, and they should be always described, in catalogues, as particularly as if they were independent works.

IV. Early printed books, without title-pages, are to be catalogued in the words of the head-title, preceded by the word [*Beginning*], in italics and between brackets; to which are to be added the words of the colophon, preceded by the word [*Ending*], in italics and between brackets.

If there be neither head-title nor colophon, such a description of the work should be given, in English, and between brackets, as may serve for its identification.

REMARK 1. Books printed before the adoption of separate title-pages are comparatively few. Most of them have been described with great minuteness by bibliographers, particularly by Maittaire, Denis, Panzer, and Hain. It will be best, in all cases, to refer to their works in cataloguing such books.

These books generally have at the beginning a head-title, which contains a sufficient description of the book, while in the colophon the place of publication, name of the printer, date, &c., are given; but sometimes the book begins with a table, or dedication, or register, and has no colophon. In such cases, not unfrequently, there is a title at the end of the table, or in the dedication. In short, so great is the variety of cases, that it would be extremely difficult, if not impossible, to give rules applicable to them all. The rule given above will, it is thought, be found sufficiently comprehensive.

V. In cataloguing Academical Dissertations, Orations, &c., the subject-matter is to be given as the title. If that be not expressed upon the title-page, it is to be supplied within brackets, if possible in the words of the author, otherwise in English and in italics. The contracted words [*Diss. Ac.*] when necessary to indicate the character of the publication, should be prefixed. The occasion may generally be omitted, except when the subject of the dissertation or oration has some special reference to it.

VI. In cataloguing Sermons, the book, chapter and verse of the *text*; the *date*, if it differs from that of publication; and the *occasion*, if a special one, are to be given. When these are not upon the title-page, they are to be supplied between brackets, and in italics.

VII. Periodical publications are to be recorded in the words of the title-page of the last complete volume; but without designation of volume or date.

The history of the publication from its commencement, including all changes of form, title, editorship, &c., is to be given in a note.

REMARK 1. This rule applies to Reviews, Magazines, &c.; not to works issued in parts, sometimes called "serials," nor to transactions of learned societies.

REMARK 2. The last title is preferred for the catalogue, because it is that by which the work is currently known, and because of the peculiar difficulty of finding complete sets of these publications. If the title be changed, it will become necessary to prepare a new one for the catalogue, and to make an addition to the note.

VIII. After the words of the title, the number of parts, volumes, fasciculi, or whatever may be the peculiar divisions of each work, is to be specified.

When nothing is said, in the title, respecting this point, if the work be divided into several portions, but the same paging continue, or, when the pages are not numbered, if the same register continue, the work is to be considered as divided into *parts* (not volumes). If the progressive number of the pages, or the register be interrupted, then each series of pages, or of letters of the register, is to be designated as a *volume*.

REMARK 1. In designating volumes when the number is not stated upon the title-page, the words Volume, Tome, Theil, Band, Deel, &c., may generally be represented by the initials alone. The numbers may be always expressed by Arabic figures. If the ordinal expression of number be used on the title-page, the figures may be given, and the ordinal termination omitted. The numbers of the first and of the last volume only are to be given, with a dash between them, thus:

V. 1-8. for Volume 1–Volume 8, i.e. Volume first–Volume eighth, or First Volume–Eighth Volume.

B. 2–22. for Zweiter Band–Zwei und zwanzigster Band.

T. 1–4. for Tomo 1–Tomo 4.

Th. 1-6. for Theil 1-Theil 6.

REMARK 2. When there is a discrepancy between the number of divisions of a work indicated on the title-page, and the actual number of volumes, as defined above, (that is, of divisions with separate pagings), the number of *pagings* should be stated;–each paging being considered a distinct volume. The paging of the preface and introductory matter is to be excepted. Appendixes, when separately paged, should be specially noticed in the title, though not reckoned as separate volumes.

IX. Next should follow the designation of the PLACE and DATE of publication. The name of the place should be given in the form and language of the title-page. If, in that, it be abbreviated, the full name should be supplied, but not translated; the added parts being between brackets.

Should either of these particulars be omitted in the title-page, the deficiency should be supplied from the knowledge of the librarian, or be noticed, in italics and between brackets.

REMARK 1. It would on many accounts be desirable to give the name of the publisher, but, as it would add very much to the labor of preparation, and considerably increase the size of the catalogue, it is thought best not to do so.

REMARK 2. In the case of early printed books, and typographical rarities, or where several editions of the same book are known to have been published in the same year and place, by different publishers, the name of the publisher should be specified.

REMARK 3. The date is to be given in Arabic figures, unless numerals be used in the title-page, in such a manner as to be on some accounts distinctive.

X. Next after the imprint should follow the designation of SIZE.

In accordance with general usage, the fold of the sheet, as folio, quarto, octavo, when it can be ascertained, is to be stated. As an additional, and more exact designation of size, the *Height and Breadth of the first full signature page* (the folio and signature lines being omitted in the measurement) are to be stated in inches and tenths, the fractions being expressed decimally.

EXPLANATION 1. The librarians should use a small square or rule, marked with inches and tenths. The first number given should represent the height, and the second, the breadth of the page. In the catalogue, the measurement would be recorded thus:–

$$8° (7.3X4.2)$$

that is, fold of sheet, 8vo; measuring, 7 inches and 3 tenths in height, by 4 inches and 2 tenths in breadth.

EXPLANATION 2. When the first signature page is not a full page, or when it has foot notes, turn to the first succeeding signature page which is full and without notes.

EXPLANATION 3. When there are no signatures, measure the first full *recto* page. If the other pages vary much from the standard page, add *irr.* for *irregular.*

EXPLANATION 4. Marginal rules and side marginal references and notes are not to be regarded in the measurement; some editions may be printed with and some without them. But such marginal references should be mentioned.

EXPLANATION 5. Catch-words generally stand upon the signature line, and are therefore not to be counted. The measurement of height should, however, comprise all printed matter below the folio line, and above the signature line. By folio line is meant that upon which stands the number of the page.

REMARKS. The designation of the form is added to the titles of books in catalogues for two purposes: to enable one to distinguish between different editions of the same book, and to convey to those who have not seen the book, some idea of its size.

The fold of the paper has been universally adopted, as the measure of size. A sheet once folded, forming two leaves, or four pages, is a folio. A sheet twice folded, forming four leaves or eight pages, is a quarto. A sheet three times folded, forming eight leaves, or sixteen pages, is an octavo. A sheet so folded as to form twelve leaves, or twenty-four pages, is a duodecimo. And so on.

But this method of designating the size of a book is inexact and frequently deceptive; because, 1st, it is not always possible to ascertain the fold; and, 2dly, the fold, when ascertained, gives no definite indication of the size or shape of the book.

In many books one can tell, at a glance, the fold of the sheet; but it is unsafe to rely upon this first impression. Examination of signatures is indispensable. Sometimes, it is necessary to examine also the water-lines and water-marks. Occasionally, all these will fail us.

Signatures are letters or figures placed at the bottom of the first page of each sheet, as guides to the binder, to denote the order of the sheets. The signatures of the different forms from folio to 32mo, would regularly be placed as follows:

> Folio, sheet, on pages 1, 5, 9, 13, 17, 21,&c.
> Quarto, sheet, on pages 1, 9, 17, 25, 33, 41,&c.
> Octavo, sheet, on pages 1, 17, 33, 49, 65, 81,&c.
> 8vo, ½ sheet, on pages 1, 9, 17, 25, 33, 41,&c.
> 12mo, sheet, on pages 1, 25, 49, 73, 97, 121,&c.
> 12mo, ½ sheet, on pages 1, 13, 25, 37, 49, 61,&c.
> 16mo, sheet, on pages 1, 33, 65, 97, 129, 161,&c.
> 16mo, ½ sheet, on pages 1, 17, 33, 49, 65, 81,&c.
> 18mo, sheet, on pages 1, 37, 73, 109, 145, 181,&c.
> 18mo, ½ sheet, on pages 1, 19, 37, 55, 73, 91,&c.
> 24mo, sheet, on pages 1, 49, 97, 145, 193, 241,&c.
> 24mo, ½ sheet, on pages 1, 25, 49, 73, 97, 121,&c.
> 32mo, sheet, on pages 1, 65, 129, 193, 257, 321,&c.
> 32mo, ½ sheet, on pages 1, 33, 65, 97, 129, 161,&c.

But sometimes the paging of the book begins in the midst of a signature; in such cases the signatures would fall on pages different from the above, throughout the book, though the intervals would be regular. Double signatures are sometimes placed upon stereotype plates, to enable printers to impose them either as octavos or duodecimos.

Besides the principal signatures, there are subordinate signatures, which, as they do not help to distinguish the size of the book, but are only used to aid the binder, are omitted in the above table.

It will be seen from this table, that the signatures are precisely the same for 8vos, in half sheets, as for 4tos; for 16mos, in half sheets, as for 8vos; for 24mos, in half sheets, as for 12mos; for 32mos, in half sheets, as for 16 mos.

Printers impose in half sheets or sheets, according to their convenience. Of course, therefore, from the signatures *alone*, it is impossible to distinguish between 4tos and 8vos, 8vos and 16mos, 12mos and 24mos, 16mos and 32mos. It is generally easy to determine the fold by the size and shape of the book, but (as we shall show hereafter) not *always*.

Signatures do not occur in the earliest printed books; but as this class of books is small, and very particularly described by Panzer, Hain, and others, there is but little difficulty in ascertaining the precise description of them.

Books may be quired in printing, that is, several sheets may be put together, like the sheets in a quire of paper. In this case the principal signature is the same as if the whole formed only one sheet. A folio may thus be undistinguishable from an 8vo, by the signatures alone.

When signatures fail us, resort may sometimes be had to the water lines, which, by holding the paper up to the light, may be seen crossing the sheet perpendicularly, in the folio, 8vo, 18mo, 24mo, and 32mo; and horizontally, in all the other forms less than 32mo; sometimes, also, in the 24mo. The water-mark is a device of the manufacturer, placed in the middle of the half sheet, and distinguishable in the same way as the water-line. In the folio, this occurs in the middle of the page; in the quarto, in the back or fold of the book; in the 8vo, at the upper and inner corner. At the present day, however, printing paper is seldom made with water-lines or water-marks.

In examining a book, all these means of determining its fold occasionally deceive the most skilful bibliographer. If sheets of paper had, from the first, been always made of the same size, there would be comparatively little difficulty. But they have always varied so much, that a very small 8vo is often in no way distinguishable, in dimensions, from a large 16mo. Many other sizes also are liable to be confounded.

The following measurements, in inches, of a leaf of folio, octavo, and 16mo, of foolscap, medium, and imperial paper, will show how impossible it would be, from the size of the book to determine the fold of the sheet, even of paper of what are called the regular sizes, particularly when the books have been cut down in binding:

	Folio,	Octavo,	16mo.
Foolscap,	13 1/4X 8 3/8,	6 5/8X4 1/4,	4 1/4X3 3/8,
Medium,	18 1/4X11 1/2,	9 1/8X5 3/4,	5 3/4X4 1/2,
Imperial,	21 7/8X15,	11 X7 1/2,	7 1/2X5 1/2,

Since the introduction of machine paper and large presses, paper is made of almost any and every size and shape, and it is no longer possible to distinguish, with accuracy, the different folds. Books, which judged by the eye, would be supposed to be quartos, are, in reality, duodecimos; books which might be supposed to be octavos, are 16mos, &c. The signatures, as we have seen, will not inform us whether a book is an 8vo, or a 16mo on half sheets. There are no water-marks to help us; nor is it possible in any way to tell.

If it be thus difficult, and often impossible, to ascertain the fold with the book before us, of what use can it be, as a designation of size, to those who have only the description? This is a difficulty which has but commenced. It is becoming more serious every year. It is more serious in America, than in other countries, for in Europe, there is much more regularity in the sizes of paper than here.

On these accounts, it has been thought desirable, if not indispensable, to introduce some new method of designating the size of books. The measurement of the printed page has seemed the readiest and most useful. The trouble of measuring is much less than might, at first sight, be supposed, and the time occupied by it is hardly worthy of consideration.

It would be, for all purposes of bibliography, better to make this the universal method of designating the size of books. It would save numberless blunders and frequent perplexity; and, upon the whole, would take less of the librarian's time, than the ordinary process of ascertaining the fold, provided that be done with exactness.

XI. In books of one volume, the body of which does not contain more than one hundred pages, the number of pages is to be specified. In applying this rule, copy the number of the last page of the body of the book, or of any addition paged continuously with it.

REMARK 1. The value of catalogues would, doubtless, be enhanced by giving the number of pages in every volume, after the manner of Dryander in the Catalogue of Sir Joseph Banks's library; or with even greater particularity, thus: *pp. xxvi+345+*XLV, meaning 26 pages of prefatory matter, 345 pages in the body of the book, and 45 pages of appendix. But the disproportionate amount of additional labor, as well as of increase in the bulk and cost of catalogues, which such enumeration and notation would demand, renders it necessary to limit the object of this rule, which is to show whether the work described be merely of pamphlet size.

REMARK 2. Prefatory matter is not to be included in the enumeration of pages. But if it be something more than a preface or introduction by the author, and deemed of sufficient importance to be added to the title, the number of pages of such prefatory matter should be included in the addition.

XII. All additions to the titles are to be printed in italics, and between brackets; to be in the English language, whatever be the language of the title; to be such only as are applicable to all copies of the edition described, and necessary for a full titular description of the book.

EXCEPTION. When parts of a name are supplied within brackets, they are to be in the vernacular of the author, whatever be the language of the title; and, if the name be used for the heading, the part supplied in the title is to correspond in typography with the rest of the name; that is, to be printed in small capitals.

REMARK 1. It is not always easy to say what additions are necessary, to render a title satisfactorily descriptive. A title is often a mere name, arbitrarily chosen by the author. It is sometimes allegorical, or embodies, in a pun, or conceit, or covert allusion, some indication of the subject-matter of the book. In such cases, it was not designed to be descriptive of the work, and could not be made so, without destroying its character. Explanations of such titles may be thought desirable; but if so, they should be given in notes, and separate from the titles themselves. A title should be the briefest possible designation of the contents of a book. It should cover everything which the book contains, but in the most general terms, without minute specifications. Mindful of this definition, we shall frequently find cases, where the title, intended to be descriptive, fails to give us what we have a right to expect. A book may be in a different language from the title-page. It may be in several languages, while the title indicates but one. It may contain an important Preface, Introduction, or Biography of the author, by another hand, not mentioned in the title. In these, and in many other cases, additions to the titles may be necessary.

REMARK 2. There are many cases, however, where it seems desirable to give further information concerning a work, than could be given within the title, under the restrictions of the preceding paragraph. The title may be a misnomer, or it may contain allusions, which it is desirable to explain. The book may be a rare and valuable one, with maps and illustrations, the number and description of which ought to be given. It may have been privately printed or limited to a small number of copies, or prohibited, or condemned to be burnt. The edition may be the *Editio princeps*, or a fac-simile of an early edition, or a surreptitious or spurious edition; or it may be identical, except in the title, with what purports to be another edition, or an independent work. These facts belong, more properly, to a bibliographical dictionary, than to a catalogue. It is proper, however, that they should be noted by cataloguers. They may, also, be printed, at the discretion of the superintendent, but generally, in the form of separate notes, rather than as additions to the titles.

REMARK 3. Peculiarities of copies, such as large paper, satin paper, vellum; also notes, autographs, cancelled leaves, substituted leaves, mutilations and alterations; binding in a different number of volumes from that indicated in the title, or ascertained by the rule already given,&c. &c.,—these, and other peculiarities or imperfections of copy, relate only to particular copies, and therefore should not be noticed in a title intended to apply to the whole edition. Every cataloguer should, however, note every such thing, after the title. The note may be printed in the catalogue of the library containing the book described, but not, usually, in the title for the General Catalogue.

HEADINGS

XIII. When the title has been transcribed in accordance with the foregoing rules, the heading is to be written above it.

This heading determines the place of the title in the alphabetical catalogue, and consists, in general, of the name of the author in its vernacular form, when the same can be represented by the letters of the English alphabet.

When the word cannot be exactly represented by English letters, the form used by the best English authorities is to be adopted.

The surname is to be printed in capitals. Christian or first names are to follow, if possible in full, printed in small capitals, and within parentheses.

XIV. When a name is variously spelled, the best authorized orthography is to be selected for the heading, and such other modes of spelling the name, as are likely to occasion difficulty, are to be added, within brackets.

Cross references are to be made from all other forms of the name, which occur in the catalogue, to the form preferred.

XV. The following rules are to be observed in cataloguing names with prefixes:

(1.) If the name has become an English surname, it is to be recorded under the prefix, which is to be accounted as part of the name.

Thus: *D'Israeli, De Morgan, De la Beche, Du Ponceau* are to be placed under *D*; *Van Buren* under *V*.

In such cases, cross-references are to be made from the principal name.

Names beginning with *Mac, O', Ap,* and *Fitz,* are to be recorded under those syllables. *Mc,* and *M',* abbreviated forms of *Mac,* are to be considered the same as if written in full.

(2.) French surnames preceded by the preposition *de* are to be catalogued under the name itself, and not under the prefix.

Thus: *Florian (Jean Pierre Claris de)* is to be placed under *F*, not under *D*; *Alembert (Jean le Rond d')* under *A*, not under *D*.

In this respect, usage is by no means uniform among French authors. Thus, Brunet places *D'Alembert* under *D*, while *Quérard*, the Editors of the "Biographic Universelle," etc., place the same name under *A*. But consistency is of the first importance, and it is decidedly best to make this rule positive, and without exceptions.

(3.) French surnames preceded by *De la*, are to be recorded under the article.

Thus: *La Pérouse (Jean François Galaup de)*, not *De la Pérouse,* nor *Pérouse; La Harpe (Jean François de)*, not *De la Harpe,* nor *Harpe.*

It is better to make this the invariable rule, although uniformity will not be found among French writers, in this particular, nor scarcely consistency in any one writer.

(4.) French names preceded by *Du* or *Des* are to be recorded under these prefixes.

Thus: *Du Halde* under *D*, not under *H*; *Des Cartes*, under *D*, not under *C*.

(5.) French names, preceded by the article *Le, La, L'*, are to be recorded under *L*.

Thus: *Le Long (Jacques)*, not *Long (Jacques le)*; *L'Héritier (Marie Jeanne)* not *Héritier (Marie Jeanne l')*.

(6.) Names with similar prefixes in other languages, are, in all cases, to be recorded under the word following the prefix, with cross-references.

Thus: *Delle Valle*, under *V*; *Della Santa*, under *S*; *Da Cunha* under *C*. So *Buch (Léopold von)*; *Recke (Elisa von der)*; *Dyck (Anton Van)*; *Pract (Joseph Basile Bernard Van)*; *Hooght (Everard van der)*; *Ess (Leander van)*.

XVI. Compound surnames, except Dutch and English, are to be entered under the initial of the first name. In Dutch and in English compound names, the last name is to be preferred.

Thus, in French, such names as *Etienne Geoffroy-Saint-Hilaire, Isidore Geoffroy-Saint-Hilaire*, should be written *Geoffroy-Saint-Hilaire (Etienne)*, *Geoffroy-Saint-Hilaire (Isidore)*. So in spanish, *Calderon de la Barca* and *Calderon y Belgrano*, should both be entered under *C*. But *François de Salignac de Lamotte Fénélon*, is universally placed under *Fénélon*, even by those who generally adhere to the above rule. There are other names, which must be considered exceptions, respecting which it seems impossible to give any invariable rule, but all difficulty must be removed by cross-references.

XVII. Works of an author who may have changed his name, or added others to it, are to be recorded under the last name, (if used in any of his publications,) with cross-references from the other names. Names that may have been altered by being used in different languages, are to be entered under their original vernacular form. But if an author has never used the vernacular form of his name in his publications, his works are to be recorded under such other form as he may have employed.

REMARK 1. Thus, *Alexander Slidell Mackenzie* should be placed under *Mackenzie*, with a cross-reference from *Slidell*. His family name was *Slidell*, but after becoming known as a writer, he assumed the name *Mackenzie*.

François Marie Aroüet de Voltaire, under *Voltaire*; because *Voltaire* is a name assumed as a surname. It is not a title, nor commonly considered part of a compound surname.

Jean Baptiste Poquelin Molière, under *Molière*. His father's name was *Poquelin*, but he added, himself, the name *Molière*, as *Aroüet* did that of *Voltaire*.

The family name of an individual is to be considered that which he has, or adopts, for himself and his descendants, rather than that which he received from his ancestors,—*his* family name, not *his father's*. Now if a man's name have been changed, by his own act, the name assumed is supposed to be that by which he wishes to be known to his contemporaries, and which he wishes to transmit to posterity. A married woman generally drops her maiden name, and assumes that of her husband. By this, therefore, she should ever after be known. If she published books under her maiden name, and afterwards under her married name, they should all be recorded under her married name, with a cross-reference from the former. It may be that she published only under her maiden name; in this case, her works should be entered under that name, followed by her married name, included within parentheses.

REMARK 2. Such changes as are referred to under this rule may generally be indicated by the mode of printing, thus:

MACKENZIE (Alexander SLIDELL).
VOLTAIRE (François Marie AROÜET de).
DACIER (*Mad.* Anne LEFÉVRE).

XVIII. The following classes of persons are to be entered under their first names, or their Christian names:

(1.) Sovereigns, and Princes of sovereign houses.

(2.) Jewish Rabbis, and Oriental writers in general.

(3.) Persons canonized. The family name, when known, is to be added within brackets.

(4.) Friars, who, by the constitution of their order, drop their surnames. But the family name, when known, should be added within brackets.

(5.) All other persons known *only* by their first names, to which, for the sake of distinction, they add those of their native places, profession, rank, &c., as, *Adamus Bremensis*, or *Adam of Bremen*.

A cross-reference should be made from any other name by which the author may be known, to that used as the heading.

XIX. Surnames of Noblemen and Dignitaries, with the exception of cases coming under the preceding rule, are to be ascertained, when not expressed, and to be used for the heading, although the person may be better known by his title, than by his name. But, in all cases where doubt would be likely to arise, cross-references should be used.

REMARK. Thus, *Home (Henry), Lord Kames*. There should be a cross-reference; thus, *Kames (Lord)*. See *Home (Henry)*. *Stanhope (Philip Dormer), Earl of Chesterfield*.
This last is one of the cases which might lead us to doubt the propriety of the rule. This author is universally known as *Chesterfield*, not as *Stanhope*. But there are other authors, who are as well known by their family names as by their titles; while the greater portion are known by their family names, much better than by their titles. A general rule is absolutely necessary, and this is thought to be the best.

XX. If it appear upon the title-page, that the work is the joint production of several writers, it is to be entered under the first named, with cross-references from the names of the others.

XXI. The complete works, or entire treatises of several authors, published together in one series, with a collective title, are to be recorded in the words of the general title of the series, and to be placed under the name of the Editor, if known; if that be not known, under the title of the collection, like anonymous works. If any work in the collection be printed with a separate title-page, and an independent paging, it is also to be recorded under its author's name, as a distinct work, with a reference to the volume of the collection in which it is to be found.

Cross-references may be made from names of authors, when they appear upon the title-page, or when their works were first published in the collection.

EXPLANATION 1. The principle established by this rule, decides the case, common among German books, of *works with double titles*, one general and the other special. Such a work must be entered twice, once under the general title, which should omit, as much as possible, what is contained in the special; and once under the special title, which should refer to the general, stating what volume of the general collection this particular volume forms.

EXPLANATION 2. This rule applies to *periodical publications*, which should be entered under the name of the Editor, if this appears upon the title-page, with a cross-reference from the name of the publication. But if the publication be issued under the direction of an association, it comes under the next rule, and is to be recorded under the name of the association, with a cross-reference from the editor's name.

REMARK. The catalogue, thus formed, will be composed of works, having each a distinct title-page and an independent pagination. Doubtless, greater convenience and usefulness might be attained by adopting a more comprehensive plan;—one, by which every distinct article in Transactions of Learned Societies, in Magazines, Reviews, and similar works, where, by the rule of the publication, the authors of the treatises are named,—should be separately entered, as if it were a book. Such an attempt is, however, at present, unadvisable. Should it, hereafter, be thought practicable to extend the rule, none of the titles which have been prepared, under this rule, will be superfluous, and none will have to be altered. It is hoped, that, within a few years, such progress may be made in the General Catalogue, as to justify the attempt at greater minuteness of registration.

XXII. Academies, institutes, associations, universities, colleges; literary, scientific, economical, eleemosynary and religious societies; national and municipal governments; assemblies, conventions, boards, corporations, and other bodies of men, under whatever name, and of whatever character, issuing publications, whether as separate works, or in a continuous series, under a general title, are to be considered and treated as the authors of all works issued by them, and in their name alone. The heading is to be the name of the body, the principal word to be the first word, not an article. A cross-reference is to be made from any important substantive or adjective, to the principal word.

EXPLANATION 1. If the name of the author appears upon the title-page of a work having a distinct title-page and paging, published by such a body, the work then comes under Rule XXI. It must be recorded twice; once under the general title, according to the above rule, and again under the name of the author, referring, if it be published in a series, to the volume of the series in which it is contained.

EXPLANATION 2. Catalogues of public libraries are to be entered under the name of the establishment; and if the name of the compiler appears upon the title-page, a cross-reference should be made from it to the principal entry.

EXPLANATION 3. When committees, or branches of a body, issue publications, the heading is to be the name of the chief, and not of the subordinate body. Thus, under *United States*, would be placed all public documents issued at the expense of the United States, whether as regular Public Documents, or by particular Departments, Bureaus, or Committees. Such titles, when they become numerous, may be classed, and conveniently arranged in the catalogue.

On the same principle, the publications of literary and other societies connected with colleges and universities are to be catalogued under the names of the colleges, &c., with cross-references from the names of the societies.

EXPLANATION 4. Under this rule, Liturgies, Prayer-books, Breviaries, Missals, &c., are to be placed under the English name of the communion, religious order or denomination, under whose authority they are prepared and published. Similar works by individuals, are to be placed under their names.

XXIII. Translations are to be entered under the heading of the original work, with a cross-reference from the name of the translator. If the name of the translator be known, and that of the author unknown, the book is to be entered, like other anonymous works, under the first word of the original title, not an article or preposition, whether the original be or be not in the library to be catalogued.

When the title of the original cannot be ascertained, or cannot be expressed in English letters, the translation is to be entered as an anonymous work, that is, under the first word of its title, not an article or preposition.

XXIV. Commentaries accompanied by the whole Text, are to be entered under the heading of the original work, with a cross-reference from the name of the commentator. If not accompanied by the Text, they are to be entered under the name of the commentator, with a cross-reference from the name of the author.

XXV. The Bible, or any part of it, in any language, is to be entered under the word "Bible."

Cross-references should be made from the names of the writers, as well as from the names of the several parts of the Bible. Both of these classes of names are to be expressed in the form adopted in the authorized English version.

XXVI. Reports of Trials are to be recorded under the name of the Reporter; or if this be not known, under the first word of the Title. There should also be cross-references, from the names of the plaintiff and of the defendant in a civil suit, and from that of the defendant in a criminal suit.

XXVII. The Respondent or defender in a thesis, is to be considered its author, except when it unequivocally appears to be the work of the Praeses.

XXVIII. Pseudonymous works are to be entered under the assumed name, followed by *pseud.*; after which may be given the name of the supposed or reputed author, with (in case of doubt) the word *probably* before it, or *?* after it.

But if the author have published any edition, continuation, or supplement under his name, the work is not to be considered pseudonymous. In such case, a cross-reference should be made from the feigned name.

EXPLANATION 1. Under pseudonyms are to be included not only fictitious names, such as *Geoffrey Crayon, Gent.*, assumed by Washington Irving, and abbreviated names, as *A. L. Mil.* for *A. L. Millin*; but also names concealed in an anagram, as *Nides*, for *Denis*; or formed from the initials of the real name, as *Talvi*, for *Theresa Adolfina Louisa Von Jacob*, and all words used fictitiously as proper names of authors.

EXPLANATION 2. Works falsely attributed, in their titles, to particular persons, are also to be treated as pseudonymous, and entered under the names of the pretended authors, with such notes as may be necessary to prevent mistake; unless some edition has been published under the name of the real author.

EXPLANATION 3. Works published with *initials*, are to be entered under the full name of the author, if he be known to have published any edition with his name; otherwise, under the *last* initial, which is to be supposed to stand for the surname, and the other letter or letters for Christian names. But if the last letter be known to stand for a title, it is not to be used for the heading.

XXIX. Anonymous works are to be entered under the first word of the title, not an article or preposition. Cross-references may be made from all words, in the title, under which such a work would be likely to be sought for, in an alphabetical catalogue.

But if the author have published any edition, continuation, or supplement under his name, the work is not to be considered anonymous.

EXCEPTION 1. An anonymous biography or personal narrative is to be entered under the name of the person, whose life or adventures form the subject of the book, if the name appears upon the title-page. But such works should in all cases be designated as anonymous.

EXCEPTION 2. An anonymous continuation, supplement, appendix or index is to be entered under the heading of the original work.

EXPLANATION 1. A book is not to be considered anonymous, when the name of the author is given in any part of it, or expressed by any distinctive description. In such case, the name of the author is to be inserted in the title, within brackets, and is to be used as the heading.

EXPLANATION 2. If it be known that the book has been *attributed* to a certain person, his name may be inserted in the title, within brackets, with such explanation as shall prevent mistake; and a cross-reference may be made from the name of the reputed author.

EXPLANATION 3. Works in which the author is described by some circumlocution, which does not serve to identify him, are to be considered anonymous.

REMARK. This rule will secure uniformity. It will relieve librarians from an almost incalculable amount of labor, perplexity and dissatisfaction. It will relieve readers from every inconvenience, except that of sometimes being obliged to look in two places for the book. On these accounts, a simple, arbitrary rule is the only one that can safely be adopted. Any rule for selecting the most prominent word of a title, or for entering a book under the name of its subject, would be found fatal to uniformity; it would greatly increase the trouble of making a catalogue; it would not render the catalogue more convenient for readers, but, in the main, much less so. The only objections to the proposed rule are, that it brings many titles under words of little significance, as a *"Brief Survey"*, a *"Succinct Narrative"*, &c., and that it brings many titles together, under such words as "Essay", "History", "Narrative", &c. These objections have been fully considered, and the rule is given with the settled conviction that the inconveniences alluded to are much less than those which would result from any other rule or set of rules, which have been proposed, or can be devised.

CROSS-REFERENCES

XXX. Cross-references,—consisting of only the word from which reference is made, the word *See*, and the name or heading referred to,—are to be made in the following instances:

(1.) From other forms of a name, than the one adopted in the heading.

(2.) From any name used by an author, or by which he may be generally known, other than the one used for the heading.

(3.) From important words in the name of any collective body, used as a heading, under Rule XXII.

(4.) From names of subordinate bodies, when a work is entered under the name of the principal body, under Rule XXII.

(5.) From the name of a supposed author of a pseudonymous work.

(6.) From titles, or designations of office, or dignity, when used upon title-pages, instead of surnames.

(7.) From the family names of persons, whose works are entered under the Christian, or first names; except sovereigns, or princes belonging to sovereign houses.

(8.) From the names of the several parts of the Bible, and of the writers of them.

(9.) From former titles of periodicals, when the publication is catalogued under an altered title, or a new editor, according to Rule VII.

XXXI. The following classes of cross-references, employed to prevent the necessity of entering titles in full, more than once, are to contain so much of the title referred to, as may be necessary to show distinctly the object of the reference. When it would be difficult to abbreviate the title, for this purpose, other words, not those of the title, may be used.

(1.) From the names of Translators, Editors, Commentators, Continuators, or other persons, named on the title-page, (or added to the title, on the principle of Rule XII.), as participating in the authorship of the work.

(2.) From the name of any person, the subject of a biography or narrative.

(3.) From the name of an author; any whole work of whom, or some considerable part of it, may be the subject of any commentary or notes, without the text.

(4.) From the name of an author, whose complete works are contained in any collection, or any considerable part of whose works have been first published in such collection, if the name be given upon the title-page.

(5.) From any word, in the title of an anonymous work, under which one would be likely to seek for the work in an alphabetical catalogue.

(6.) From the name of a supposed author of an anonymous work.

(7.) From the names of the plaintiff and of the defendant, in the report of a civil suit; and from the name of the defendant, in that of a criminal suit.

(8.) From the name of a former editor of a periodical, when the publication is catalogued under the name of a new editor, according to Rule VII.

ARRANGEMENT

XXXII. The order of the Headings will be determined by the plan of the catalogue, whether alphabetical, classed, or chronological.

XXXIII. The Titles are immediately to follow the headings; and within the divisions and sub-divisions given below, the arrangement is to be chronological. Editions without date, and those of which the date cannot be ascertained, even by approximation, are to precede all those bearing date, or of which the date can be supplied, either positively or by approximation. The latter are to follow, according to their date, whether apparent in any part of the book, or supplied. Editions by the same editor, or such as are expressly stated to follow a specific text or edition, and editions with the same notes or commentary, to succeed each other, in their chronological order, immediately after the entry of that which is, or is considered to be, the earliest.

XXXIV. Titles, which occur under the name of an author, are to be arranged in the following order:

(1.) Collections of all the works.

a. Those without translations, whether with or without notes, commentaries, lives, or other critical apparatus.

b. Those with translations.

Editions with only one translation. Those with a Latin translation are to be placed first; next those with an English; and then those with a translation into any other language, in the alphabetical order of the English name of such language.

Editions with several translations into different languages. Those are to be entered first, which have the fewest number of translations. Among those having the same number of translations, the alphabetical order of the first of the languages employed is to be followed.

c. Translations without the text. These are to be arranged among themselves according to the principles laid down for translations with the text.

(2.) Partial collections, containing two or more works. Those which contain the greatest number of works are to precede. The arrangement of the whole is to be, in other respects, according to the principles laid down for collections of all the works.

(3.) Selections or collected fragments. Those from all the works are to precede those from several works, and the whole to be arranged according to the foregoing principles.

(4.) Separate works. These are to succeed each other alphabetically. Entire portions of a separate work are to follow immediately after the work itself. The different editions and translations are to be arranged according to the foregoing principles.

(5.) Entire portions of a separate work, when the work itself does not occur.

XXXV. Works placed under the names of collective bodies (according to Rule XXII,) are, in general, to be arranged in alphabetical order; but works forming part of a series are not to be separated, although that series be interrupted, or the title changed; and works published by branches or subordinate bodies, are to be separately arranged and placed under sub-headings, which should be printed in a distinctive type.

XXXVI. Cross-References are to be placed after all other entries under the heading, and in alphabetical order of the names referred to.

XXXVII. The entries under the word *Bible*, are to be arranged in the following order; subject in other respects to the principles laid down in Rule XXXIV, except that, in each of the following classes, editions with the text alone are to precede those with commentaries.

(1.) The Old and New Testaments with or without the Apocrypha.

(2.) The Old Testament.

(3.) Detached parts of the Old Testament, in the same order in which they are arranged in the English authorized version of the Scriptures.

(4.) The New Testament.

(5.) Detached parts of the New Testament.

(6.) Apocryphal books.

MAPS, ENGRAVINGS, MUSIC

XXXVIII. Maps, Charts, Engravings and Music, (except when published in volumes,) are not to be included in catalogues of Books. Separate catalogues of these should be constructed upon the general principles of the preceding rules.

(1.) In cataloguing MAPS AND CHARTS, the full title is to be given, including the names of surveyors, compilers, engravers, publishers, &c.; date and place of publication; and number of sheets composing the map. Each edition is to be separately recorded, and the separate title of each sheet, when it varies from the general title. The titles of sub-sketches are to be introduced at the close of the main title, within brackets, and to be given in full, including authorship, scale and size.

(2.) The scale is to be given in all cases. When not stated on the map, it is, if possible, to be derived from it.

(3.) The size of the map, within the *neat-line* of the border, is to be given in inches and tenths. When a map has no printed border, the measure of the limits of printed surface is to be given.

(4.) The price, if stated on the map, should be copied.

(5.) All important peculiarities of copy, such as the kind of paper, and whether backed, folded, bound, on rollers, &c., should be mentioned in a note.

The titles thus prepared are to be arranged under the names of the countries, or divisions of the earth's surface delineated in the maps; and these names are to be disposed in alphabetical order, with the cross-references necessary to facilitate research.

(6.) ENGRAVINGS are to be recorded under the names of the engravers, with cross-references from those of the painters or designers. The date, and the name of the publisher, if found upon the print, should also be given. The size of the print, in inches and tenths, should also be stated. If the copy be an artists' proof, or a remarkably good impression of a valuable engraving, the fact should be stated in a note.

(7.) MUSIC is to be entered under the name of the composer. If the work have a distinctive title, there should be a cross-reference from that.

EXCEPTIONAL CASES

XXXIX. Cases not herein provided for, and exceptional cases, requiring a departure from any of the preceding rules, are to be decided upon by the superintendent.

Part III

Bibliography

JEWETT'S MANUSCRIPTS

Few of Jewett's manuscript letters have survived to this day. Some few will be found in the archives of Brown University; some in the Boston Public Library; and a few others in scattered collections. The letter to Seth Hastings Grant reprinted above is from the Grant Papers in the American Library Association Archives now housed in the Archives of the University of Illinois.

JEWETT'S PUBLISHED WORKS

Jewett was not particularly prolific if one compares him with such later worthies as Winsor, Poole, and Dewey. However, he did produce a sizeable body of material. The following is a list of his writings.

The Close of the Late Rebellion in Rhode Island. An Extract from a Letter by a Massachusetts Man Resident in Providence. Providence: B. Cranston & Co., 1842. This work was published anonymously.

Preface to the Catalogue of the Library of Brown University. Providence, 1843. This preface contains a history of the Library, a description of the methods used in preparing the catalog, and a copy of the Rules and Regulations of the Library.

Facts and Considerations Relative to Duties on Books; Addressed to the Library Committee of Brown University. Printed by Order of the Committee. Providence: J. F. Moore, printer, 1846.

"Reports of the Assistant Secretary in Charge of the Library," in the *Annual Reports of the Board of Regents of the Smithsonian Institution*, 1846-1855. Washington, 1847-1856.

Notices of Public Libraries in the United States of America. Washington, 1851. This volume was first published as an appendix to the *Annual Report* of the Smithsonian for 1849, and then was issued in 1851 with an added title page.

"A Plan for Stereotyping Catalogues by Separate Titles and for Forming a General Stereotyped Catalogue of Public Libraries in the United States," *Proceedings* of the American Association for the Advancement of Science, 1850.

On the Construction of Catalogues of Libraries and Their Publication by Means of Separate, Stereotyped Titles. With Rules and Examples. Washington, Smithsonian Institution, 1852. This work was published in a second edition in 1853.

"Reports of the Superintendent," in the *Annual Reports of the Trustees of the Public Library of the City of Boston* 1858-1868.

Jewett also issued two major catalogues while he was Superintendent of the Boston Public Library: *Index to the Catalogue of a Portion of the Public Library of the City of Boston, Arranged in the Lower Hall* . . . Boston: Press of G. C. Rand and Avery, 1858; and *Index to the Catalogue of Books in the Upper Hall of the Public Library of the City of Boston*. Boston: G. C. Rand and Avery, 1861.

SECONDARY PUBLICATIONS

GENERAL STUDIES

Borome, Joseph. *Charles Coffin Jewett*. Chicago: American Library Association, 1951.

"Charles Coffin Jewett," *Dictionary of American Biography* V: 65-66.

Guild, Reuben Aldridge. "Memorial Sketch of Prof. Charles Coffin Jewett," *Library Journal* 12 (1887): 507-511.

EARLY LIFE AND THE YEARS AT BROWN

Bronson, Walter C. *The History of Brown University, 1764-1914*. Providence: The University, 1914.

Coleman, Peter J. *The Transformation of Rhode Island, 1790-1860*. Providence: Brown University Press, 1963.

Jewett, Charles Coffin. *Preface to Catalogue of the Library of Brown University*. Providence, 1843.

Thompson, J. Earl. "Abolitionism and the Theological Education at Andover," *New England Quarterly* 47 (1974): 238-261.

Williams, Daniel Day. *The Andover Liberals; A Study in American Theology*. New York: Columbia University Press, 1941.

THE SMITHSONIAN INSTITUTION LIBRARY

Adler, Cyrus. "The Smithsonian Library," in George Brown Goode, ed., *The Smithsonian Institution, 1846-1896; the History of its First Half Century*. Washington, 1897. pp. 265-302.

Billings, John Shaw, "The Influence of the Smithsonian Institution Upon the Development of Libraries, the Organization and Work of Societies, and the Publication of Scientific Literature in the United States," in George Brown Goode, ed., *The Smithsonian Institution, 1846-1896; the History of its First Half Century*. Washington, 1897. pp. 815-22.

Cole, John Young. "Ainsworth Spofford and the National Library." Ph.D. dissertation, George Washington University, 1971.

Johnston, William Dawson. "The Smithsonian Institution and the Plans for a National Library," in his *History of The Library of Congress, Volume 1, 1800-1864*. Washington: Government Printing Office, 1904, Chapter 10.

Rhees, William Jones, ed. *The Smithsonian Institution; Documents Relative to its Origin and History, 1835-1899. . . .* Washington: Government Printing Office, 1901.

Spofford, Ainsworth Rand. "Relation Between the Smithsonian Institution and the Library of Congress," in George Brown Goode, ed., *The Smithsonian Institution, 1846-1896; the History of its First Half Century*. Washington, 1897. pp. 823-32.

THE LIBRARIANS' CONFERENCE OF 1853

Fletcher, William I. *Public Libraries in America*. Boston: Little, Brown and Co., 1889.

Green, Samuel Swett. *The Public Library Movement in the United States. . . .* Boston: The Boston Book Company, 1919.

Holley, Edward G. *Raking the Historic Coals; The ALA Scrapbook of 1876*. Beta Phi Mu, 1967.

Krummel, Donald W. "The Library World of *Norton's Literary Gazette*," in David Kaser, ed., *Books in America's Past; Essays Honoring Rudolph H. Gjelsness*. Charlottesville: University of Virginia Press, 1966. pp. 238-65.

Magrath, Sister Gabriella. "Library Conventions of 1853, 1876 and 1877," *Journal of Library History* 8 (1973): 52-69.

Poole, William Frederick. "Conference of Librarians: Address of the President," *Library Journal* 11 (1886): 199-204.

Utley, George Burwell. *The Librarians' Conference of 1853*. Chicago: American Library Association, 1951.

THE BOSTON PUBLIC LIBRARY

Borome, Joseph. "The Life and Letters of Justin Winsor." Ph.D. dissertation, Columbia University, 1950.

Buchanan, Jean Briscoe. "Early Directions of the Boston Public Library and the Genesis of an American Public Library Psychology." Master's thesis, Southern Connecticut State College, 1962.

Collier, Francis G. "A History of the American Public Library Movement Through 1880." Ph.D. dissertation, Harvard University, 1953.

Haraszti, Zoltan. "A Hundred Years Ago," *Boston Public Library Quarterly* 4 (1952): 115-24.

Harris, Michael H. "The Purpose of the American Public Library; A Revisionist Interpretation of History," *Library Journal* 98 (1973): 2509-2514.

Harris, Michael H. *The Role of the Public Library in American Life: A Speculative Essay*. University of Illinois Graduate Library School, Occasional Papers, January 1975.

Harris, Michael H., and Gerard Spiegler. "Everett, Ticknor and the Common Man; The Fear of Societal Instability as the Motivation for The Founding of the Boston Public Library," *Libri* 24 (1974): 249-276.

Harwell, Richard, and Roger Michener. "As Public as the Town Pump," *Library Journal* 99 (1974): 959-63.

Shera, Jesse H. *Foundations for the Public Library: The Origins of the Public Library Movement in New England, 1629-1855*. Chicago: University of Chicago Press, 1949.

Tyack, David B. *George Ticknor and the Boston Brahmins*. Cambridge: Harvard University Press, 1967.

Wadlin, Horace G. *The Public Library of the City of Boston; A History*. Boston: Printed by the Trustees, 1911.

Whitehill, Walter Muir. *The Boston Public Library: A Centennial History*. Cambridge: Harvard University Press, 1956.

JEWETT'S CATALOGS

"[A review of the] Catalogue of the Library of Brown University," *North American Review* 122 (1844): 227-236.

Lehnus, Donald J. *Milestones in Cataloging; Famous Catalogers and Their Writings, 1835-1969*. Littleton, Colorado: Libraries Unlimited, 1974.

Palmer, Vivian D. "A Brief History of Cataloging Codes in the United States, 1852-1949," Master's thesis, University of Chicago, 1963.

Ranz, Jim, "The Age of Jewett, 1850-1875. . . ." in his *The Printed Book Catalogue in American Libraries, 1723-1900*. Chicago: American Library Association, 1964. Chapters 3 and 4.

INDEX

Abolitionism, Jewett on, 8-9
Acquisitions, Jewett on, 89-97
Ampère, André-Marie, 133
Andover Theological Seminary
    Catalogue of the Library, 9-10
    Jewett as a student there, 8-10
    Jewett as a student librarian there, 9-10

Bacon, Francis, 133
Barnard, Henry, 33
Bibliography, Jewett on, 87, 128
Bibliomaniac, 23, 118
Bodleian Library, 105, 124
Bodley, Thomas, 105
Boston Public Library, 38-43
Booktrade, in mid-nineteenth century
  Europe and America, 16-17, 66-76,
  83-84
British Museum, Jewett's assessment of,
  17-18, 90, 134-35, 137
Brown University
    and the Dorr War, 12-14
    Jewett as a student there, 5-8
    Jewett and the University Library, 11-19,
    59-76
    and the literary societies' libraries, 7-8
Brown, William Lawton, 8

Card catalog, at the Boston Athenaeum,
  138
Cataloging practice, 14-16
    Jewett on, 59-65, 93-94, 98-103, 110,
    123-55
*Catalogue of the Andover Theological
  Seminary Library* (1838), 9-10
Catalogue of the Brown University Library
  (1843), 14-16

Choate, Rufus, and the Smithsonian Institu-
  tion, 21-23, 36, 121
Cogswell, Joseph Green, 17, 98, 114
Coleridge, Samuel Taylor, 133
Collection development. *See* Acquisitions.
College libraries, as defined and described
  by Jewett, 46 (note 27)
Conference of Librarians. *See* Librarians'
  Conference.
Copyright deposit, at the Smithsonian, 78,
  89, 92-93, 104-108

De Quincey, Thomas, quoted by Jewett,
  82-83
Dorr War, 12-14
Duties on books, Jewett on, 18-19, 66-76

Edinburgh Review, cited by Jewett, 134
Edwards, Edward, cited by Jewett, 79
Everett, Edward, 98
Exchanges, Jewett on, 91, 108

*Facts and Considerations Relative to Duties
  on Books* (1846), 18-19, 66-76
Fletcher, William I., assesses Jewett's importance, 55 (note 134)
Folsom, Charles
    elected President of the Librarians'
    Conference of 1853, 35
    declines the honor, 35
    introduces resolutions honoring Jewett,
    36-37, 128-30
    mentioned, 114, 116, 138

Goddard, William, and the Dorr War, 13
Grant, Seth Hastings, 33-35, 112
 Jewett's letter to, 113-15
Guild, Reuben A.
 at the Librarians' Conference of 1853,
  35
 remembers Jewett, 43, 44 (note 1), 129

Hale, Edward Everett, 33, 98, 125
Harris, T. W., 33
Harvard University Library, catalog, 9
Haven, Samuel F., 35, 98, 120, 129
Hayward, Elijah, at the Librarians' Con-
 ference of 1853, 36, 123
Henry, Joseph, 23-32, 36, 38-39

Irish, 39-40

Jackson, Andrew, 20
Jewett, Charles Coffin
 childhood and family background, 4
 early education, 5
 student at Brown, 5-8
 student librarian at Brown, 7-8
 student at Andover, 9-10
 student librarian at Andover, 8-10
 appointed librarian at Brown, 11-19
 his *Catalogue* of the Brown University
  Library (1843), 14-16, 59-65
 his book buying tour of Europe, 16-18
 his views on duties on books, 18-19,
  66-76
 Librarian at the Smithsonian Institution,
  23-32, 77-111
 his stereotype catalog scheme, 29-31, 94,
  98-103, 120-130
 his Rules for a catalog, 131-155
 at the Librarians' Conference, 33-37,
  115-30
 at the Boston Public Library, 39-43
 his death, 42
 reputation assessed, 42-43
 on reading, 82-83, 119
 compares American and European
  libraries, 80-85
Jewett, John Punchard, 4
Jewett, Paul, 4

Leibnitz, Gottfried Wilhelm von, 133
Librarians, Jewett's definition of, 34, 113
Librarians' Conference of 1853, 33-37
 Jewett's letter to Grant, 113-15

Librarians' Conference of 1853 (cont'd)
 Jewett's Presidential Address, 116-19
 Jewett's speech on the Smithsonian
  Institution and its catalog, 120-30
Library of Congress, 23, 53, 114, 125-26,
 128
Literary society libraries
 at Brown, 7-8
 general description of, 45 (note 12)
Livermore, George, 98
Ludwig, Hermann E., 78
Lyell, Charles, 40

Meacham, James, 53 (note 115)
"Mud catalogue." *See* Stereotype catalog.

National library, 20-32
 Jewett on, 77-111, 120-30
National union catalog, Jewett's plans, 29-30,
 93-94, 98-103, 123-30
New York Daily Times, on the Librarians'
 Conference of 1853, 34-35
New York Mercantile Library, 33
North American Review
 assesses Jewett's catalog of 1843, 15-16
 cited by Senator Choate, 22-23
 comments on the Smithsonian, 53
  (note 115)
 on librarianship, 31
Norton, Charles, 31, 33, 53, 107, 112, 114,
 122
Norton's Literary Gazette, 31, 33, 107, 117,
 122
Notices of Public Libraries (1851), 26-29
 Jewett's remarks on, 50-51, 79-80

Owen, Robert Dale, 49 (note 71)

Panizzi, Antonio, and Jewett, 17, 135, 138
Philanthropy, Jewett on, 90-91, 109
Philermenian Society at Brown University,
 7-8, 45-46
Polk, James K., 23
Poole, William Frederick
 assessment of Jewett's "mud catalogue," 30
 comments on the Librarians' Conference
  of 1853, 33, 37
 makes Jewett the subject of his ALA
  presidential address, 42-43
Providence, R. I., Dorr War, 12-14
 Riot of 1831, 5
Public libraries, 27-28, 39-40, 81

Reading, Jewett on, 82-83, 119
Rules for cataloging, Jewett on, 131-155

Smith, Lloyd P., 33, 116, 129
Smithson, James, 20-21
Smithsonian Institution, 20-32, 36, 77-111, 120-30
Spofford, Ainsworth Rand, 53 (note 117), 89
Stereotype catalog, 29-31
    Poole's definition, 30

Stereotype catalog (cont'd)
    reviewed at the Librarians' Conference of 1853, 34-36, 94, 98-103, 113-14
Stevens, Henry, 17

Tappen, Benjamin, 21
Tariffs on books. *See* Walker Tariff.
Taylor, Oliver A., 9-10, 15, 61
Ticknor, George, 17, 39-42, 95

Walker Tariff, 18-19, 66-76
Wayland, Francis, 5-6, 11-14, 45
Winsor, Justin, 31, 55 (note 132)